MW00811590

"*Lift Your Eyes* by Whitney Newby is a balm for the heart of every weary young mom. In this beautifully crafted book based on Psalm 121, readers will find an abundance of biblical encouragement reminding them that even in the most challenging motherhood moments, God's sustaining love is always present. The vulnerable stories and heartfelt insights inspire mothers to keep going, trust in God's unwavering support, and believe that He will continually fill their cup. The book includes practical applications to nurture an atmosphere of hope and truth in the heart of every mother.

Whitney's lovely artwork adds a layer of whimsy, perfectly complementing the uplifting content. Her illustrations bring the promises of Psalm 121 to life in a way that soothes the tired mama's soul. This book is a treasure for any mother seeking solace, and it's a gentle reminder that they are never alone in the sacred calling of loving our children for the Lord."

—**Jennifer Pepito**, author of *Habits for a Sacred Home* and Peaceful Press founder

"In *Lift Your Eyes,* Whitney reminds us that while motherhood is refining, it's doing a beautiful work in us for our good and God's glory. Each page of this book is filled with wisdom, encouragement, and practical application for the common difficulties we face in motherhood. Her words remind us how to think biblically about our situations and keep our eyes fixed on the horizon and the glory of Christ."

—**Laura Wifler**, author, podcaster, and coauthor of *Risen Motherhood* and *Gospel Mom*

"Whitney's words are a breath of fresh air to weary moms who need to be reminded to lift their eyes to Jesus amid the mundane, monotony, and messy of motherhood. Each devotion is short (perfect for busy moms!) but packs a powerful punch of encouragement. The watercolor art woven throughout the pages perfectly complements Whitney's message that while motherhood is often hard and exhausting, there is so much beauty to be found if we will but look for it."

—**Crystal Paine**, *New York Times* bestselling author and mom of six

"In *Lift Your Eyes,* Whitney Newby is there for tired moms, offering gospel-driven hope when we need it most. Lovely watercolor illustrations complement Scripture-rich reflections, making this devotional a refreshing gift for any mother."

 —**Hunter Beless**, author and founder of Journeywomen Ministries

"With much warmth and wisdom, *Lift Your Eyes* encourages mothers to remember the source of their help as they are in the thick of motherhood. Using Psalm 121 as the framework for how moms can lift their eyes from the daily realities of motherhood to the character and steadfast love of the Lord, Whitney shows her readers how every promise of God finds its 'Yes' and 'Amen' in Jesus, and that in Him we have all that we need for the journey in all ages and stages of motherhood."

 —**Courtney Tracy**, author of *Putting Jesus First: A 21-day Devotional Journey Through Colossians*

"The eyes of a mom are always darting around: ahead at all she has to tackle, all over to assess the needs of her kids, to the left to see how she's measuring up, down at the messes she has to clean, and in the mirror lamenting the toll of motherhood. *Lift Your Eyes* invites moms to fix their gaze on something more life giving—and I don't just mean the watercolor illustrations. With clear and accessible writing as beautiful as her art, Whitney vulnerably, authentically, and sincerely shares the good news of the gospel for the good, bad, ugly, and ordinary days of motherhood in a way that will redeem the way you see it all."

 —**Abbey Wedgeworth**, mom of three, author of *Held* and the *Training Young Hearts* series

"When tired, stressed, or depressed, we are tempted to fix our eyes in any place but the right place. In *Lift Your Eyes,* my friend Whitney lovingly, joyfully, and faithfully inspires hard-working moms to lift their eyes to the One who helps, the Lord who made heaven and earth. Though this book is designed to encourage moms, its message is the refrain of every Christian's life—we are loved, saved, and held, and as we live this sometimes-turbulent life, we will lift our eyes to the One who has paid for and continuously provides for all our needs."

 —**Ryan Welsh**, lead pastor at Restoration Church

LIFT YOUR EYES

WHITNEY NEWBY

HARVEST HOUSE PUBLISHERS
EUGENE, OREGON

Cover design by Faceout Studio
Cover images © Yuliia Druzenko / Shutterstock
Interior design by Janelle Courey
Original artwork by Whitney Newby

Lyrics for "Yet Not I But Through Christ in Me" used with permission.

For bulk, special sales, or ministry purchases, please call 1-800-547-8979.
Email: CustomerService@hhpbooks.com

LIFT YOUR EYES

Copyright © 2025 by Whitney Newby
Published by Harvest House Publishers
Eugene, Oregon 97408
www.harvesthousepublishers.com

ISBN 978-0-7369-8931-2 (Hardcover)
ISBN 978-0-7369-8932-9 (eBook)

Library of Congress Control Number: 2024935695

Printed in Colombia

24 25 26 27 28 29 30 31 32 33 / NI / 10 9 8 7 6 5 4 3 2 1

For women who long to know, love, trust,
and obey Christ on the journey of motherhood:

"Those who look to him are radiant, and
their faces shall never be ashamed."

PSALM 34:5

And for Liam, Lanie, Bear, and Beckham:
You have spurred me to lift my eyes to our good
and glorious Shepherd as I seek to shepherd
your hearts. I pray you'll trust and treasure him
who keeps you now and forever.

To mothers who are weary and need rest;
to all who mourn and long for comfort;
to all who feel worthless and wonder if God cares;
to all who fail and desire strength;
to all who sin and need a Savior;
to all who hunger and thirst for righteousness;
and to whoever will listen—
may the words of this book offer encouragement
in the name of Jesus Christ, our Lord.[1]

Contents

Foreword

SALLY CLARKSON

*Everyone then who hears these words of mine and does them will
be like a wise man who built his house on the rock. And the rain
fell, and the floods came, and the winds blew and beat on that
house, but it did not fall, because it had been founded on the rock.*

MATTHEW 7:24-25

When I was a young single missionary living in Austria, one of my favorite retreats was a village in the lake district in the Austrian Alps. Hallstatt is a thousand-year-old town tucked between a towering mountainside and a deep lake. To get there, I had to take a train from Vienna. I would step off the train onto a small platform standing all by itself on the other side of the lake, then walk a few steps to a dock where a boat would take me the rest of the way to Hallstatt. As I stood at the back of the tiny boat, with the soft spray of the lake blowing in my face, I always noticed the remains of a small rock castle built on the side of the mountain.

One weekend I had taken my mother and a friend to visit this favorite retreat. We dined on a lovely deck outside our quaint hotel, which fronted the water, then retired to our rooms. Within an hour, however, a ferocious storm engulfed the whole area. The electricity in the town suddenly went off. We looked out our third-story windows and saw, in the darkness, that the deck where we had recently eaten was now flooded with violent, tossing waves.

As we peered fearfully across the lake, everything seemed to be moving sideways and up and down. The high winds were blowing the torrents of rain sideways, the trees were bent over, and everything seemed to be caught up in the violence of the storm. An enormous flash of lightning illuminated the black sky. And suddenly I saw the outline of the stone castle, standing constant amid a storm that was shaking everything else to its core.

I have never forgotten the sense of strength and solidity I felt, gazing at that old structure that had not been daunted by centuries of such storms. It has become to me a picture of what God has created a home to be.

Women are created to be home builders, ("The wisest of women builds her house," Proverbs 14:1). But the reality is, so many storms come our way, trying to destroy our homes and tear them apart.

A faithful mom is not someone who is perfect in following all her ideals, but one who is willing to believe that God is good, to believe his Word and that he will help us through all the ups and downs. A mama who puts one foot in front of the other day after day, year after year.

The habit of coming to God every day, seeking him, to listen and ponder his ways and engage in his truth, is the most profound action that will shape a mother's life and the life of her children who are observing her ways.

I hardly need to say I was not perfect. Stressful crisis seasons kept me from this habit at times. Yet reading God's Word and praying was essential to my ability to continue taking one more step in the direction of my own ideals—the fuel for my strength when life was exhausting.

If I am serious about God, I must be serious about investing in him and his Word. Others need the truth he teaches me.

More voices and messages invade the sound waves of our brains today than ever. Living in a melting pot of cultures, where all religions, values, and morals drift together and are said to be equal; where all varieties of moral behavior are validated and find acceptance; where television, film, and the internet smudge the clear borders of truth every day, means the call to teach children has never been more profoundly necessary.

In my own journey as a mama, I needed the wisdom and insight of other women who had gone before me. I longed to be understood as well as coached by other wise companions who were in the journey as well.

When I had the privilege of reading Whitney's book, I knew immediately that her stories and admonitions would be such an encouragement to so many women who long for inspiration and companionship in their lives as moms. She writes her own stories so personally that we feel like we are with her in her everyday life, but she then always points us to God and his Word to give us strength to hold on to. She harkens back to the foundation upon which we can build our homes. We need the infusion of inspiration while also needing to feel understood by those who have walked this demanding role of motherhood before us.

Whitney comes alongside us as a friend who has learned the secret of building her own life, her own house, on the strength and shelter of God's Word. In each page, you will feel understood. Yet, you will also leave having hope that God sees you, loves you, and will walk with you in each experience and trial of your life. I know that many will be held by these words. And you will sense that you can walk confidently through the myriad demanding details of a mother's life, but with hope, the companionship of God, and wisdom to follow his ways.

Introduction

On a crisp October day in 2012, we brought our first baby home from the hospital. As I cradled him in my arms, I was overcome with a flood of emotions—wonder, adoration, and a nagging sense of trepidation. The weight of my responsibilities as a brand-new mom felt almost crushing. I couldn't help but wonder about my baby's future: Would he learn to breastfeed and sleep through the night? Would he develop as he should? Would he grow to be kind and respectful? Would he break my heart? My thoughts quickly turned inward, and I felt vulnerable and uncertain. As I gazed at my little one, I was hopelessly in love, but I also felt weak, hormonal, and already exhausted. I knew the journey ahead would be the greatest adventure of my life, but at the time, the questions I had about my ability to mother him seemed to outweigh all the others. How would I know what to do when he started crying? Would we be able to bond? Did I have what it takes to be the mom he deserves?

Now, over a decade into mothering, I still face questions. Although I learned to meet my babies' needs and to survive on less sleep, I am still often overwhelmed by the job of shepherding the lives of my four young children. When the needs of motherhood press in on me, it isn't always my first inclination to lift my eyes to Christ. Instead, I tend to gaze at the "hills" of motherhood: never-ending mountains of laundry, toddler tantrums, fears about the future, and the weight of comparison. But when we fix our eyes on the needs right in front of us, we forget that our God stands ready to help. We forget that he is as close as our shadow (Psalm 121:5). I am writing this book in real time as a mother who is daily learning what it means to lift my eyes to Christ—and not only my eyes, but my heart, my voice, and every part of my being. By doing so, I remind myself that he is with me, he is for me, and he will keep me every step of the way.

The writers of the Psalms understood our natural human inclination to fret and worry. In Psalm 121, the psalmist sings, "I lift up my eyes to the hills. From where does my help come?" He immediately answers his own question by singing in the face of his fears: "My help comes from the LORD, who made heaven and earth" (verses 1-2).

Psalm 121 is part of a collection of 15 psalms called the Songs of Ascent that Jewish pilgrims traditionally sang while traveling the uphill road to Jerusalem to attend three annual festivals in the temple (Exodus 23:14-19). They sang these songs as a prayer of protection as they crossed a steep, narrow path filled with potential dangers that loomed in the hills. But these pilgrim songs weren't only intended for the rocky road to Jerusalem; the songs shaped their spiritual journey as well. These pilgrims were traveling to the very presence of God, who dwelled in the temple on Mount Zion.

So what does this have to do with mothers?

On our parenting journey, we often find ourselves stretched thin and feeling weak. Few things expose our need for a Helper as profoundly as motherhood. Those hard days lead us to ask, "Will God really provide everything I need? Is he enough?" And what we need—more than a fresh cup of coffee, an hour alone, or more sleep—is to know the Source of our help. We need his living Word to shape our perspective, remind us of our identity, and equip us for the holy work before us. We need *him*.

Each of the eight verses of Psalm 121 reveals an aspect of God's character. Using this psalm as a framework, we will learn how to "lift our eyes" from the daily realities of motherhood to the steadfast love of the Lord. Each of the eight sections of this devotional begins with a short commentary about one of God's attributes seen in the text, followed by five devotions intended to meet you in your everyday circumstances. And when we realize that all of Scripture is ultimately about Christ (Luke 24:27; John 5:39), we will see that Jesus is the fulfillment of this psalm. In light of the redemptive work he has done on our behalf, we know that Christ himself is our Help, our Provider, the God who Sees, our Protector, our Keeper, our Comfort, our Shepherd, and our Sustainer.

You can read this book from beginning to end or choose a devotion that aligns with your current season or struggle. But all the devotions come together as one, helping to shape our understanding of God's steadfast love for us.

As moms, we spend a lot of time looking down: at our phones, at the toddler at our feet, at our never-ending to-do lists. We also gaze to the side, envious of what others have. We might even look behind us, nostalgic about the past or ahead to the future, hoping life will someday feel more manageable than it does right now. But what if God, through his Word, is gently placing his hand under our chins and lifting our eyes upward toward him? When we fix our eyes on him and remember all that he has done, we can move forward with purpose, knowing that he is with us and has promised to help us every step of the way.

I pray that this book will remind and equip you to raise your eyes to your steady, unchanging God, who promises to keep you because of what Christ has done. He watches, guards, and protects you on the difficult days you want to escape, the glorious days you wish would never end, and every ordinary day from now to eternity. In him, we find the life-sustaining rest, provision, strength, and wisdom we need for our journey as moms.

Where does our help come from? It comes from the Lord. Let's lift our eyes to him.

PSALM 121

A Song of Ascents

I lift up my eyes to the hills.
    From where does my help come?
My help comes from the Lord,
    who made heaven and earth.
He will not let your foot be moved;
    he who keeps you will not slumber.
Behold, he who keeps Israel
    will neither slumber nor sleep.
The Lord is your keeper;
    the Lord is your shade on your right hand.
The sun shall not strike you by day,
    nor the moon by night.
The Lord will keep you from all evil;
    he will keep your life.
The Lord will keep
    your going out and your coming in
    from this time forth and forevermore.

For centuries, Psalm 121 has given God's people hope for life's journey. Jewish pilgrims sang these words while treading the treacherous path to Jerusalem. David Livingstone, a missionary and explorer, read it aloud as he set out for the uncharted territory of central Africa in 1840.[1] Even today, this psalm hangs in the rooms of laboring Jewish mothers as they usher new life into the world.[2] Psalm 121 is easy to memorize and powerful to recall when the path gets steep, and you need to be reminded of who God is. Below, you'll find a memorization technique that uses the first letter of each word to help you commit this psalm to memory. Read Psalm 121 in full, then use the first-letter technique to practice reciting it a few times each day until it becomes the truth ringing in your heart.

ILUMETTH. FWDMHC?
MHCFTL, WMHAE.
HWNLYFBM; HWKYWNS.
B, HWKIWNSNS.
TLIYK; TLIYSOYRH.
TSSNSYBD, NTMBN.
TLWKYFAE; HWKYL.
TLWKYGOAYCIFTTFAF.

PART ONE

The Lord Is Your Help

I lift up my eyes to the hills.
From where does my help come?

PSALM 121:1

A ncient Israelites had reasons to fear as they traveled from their homes in rural villages to the city of Jerusalem every year for one of three major feasts. Their trek was treacherous and fraught with danger: blistering heat, wild animals, and thieves hiding in the hills. These men and women must have felt acutely vulnerable and helpless.

As a mother, you can probably relate to feeling fragile and afraid at times. Though you may have never physically traveled the rocky path to Jerusalem, you are certainly familiar with the vulnerability the psalmist describes. Our journey as parents is full of steep hills and low valleys, and you may feel exhausted or worried about raising your precious children in an increasingly divided world. These feelings reveal your need for a Helper.

As we dive into a study of Psalm 121 and focus on who God has promised to be for us, we will find that he doesn't guarantee a smooth path. He offers something far better: his helpful, comforting, protective, sustaining presence. He never leaves us to walk the journey of motherhood alone.

When Peter saw Jesus miraculously walking on the Sea of Galilee, he asked if he could walk on the water too (Matthew 14:22-33). Jesus granted his request and beckoned, "Come," and Peter climbed over the side of the boat. We can imagine Peter's eyes fixed on Jesus as he took those first faith-filled steps on the water. But it wasn't long before Peter's attention shifted to his situation—he was far from solid ground. When he saw the wind and began to sink, Peter cried out to Jesus, pleading, "Lord, save me" (verse 30).

We know what it feels like to look around at our own circumstances and to sink into a pit of worry, doubt, and despair. The enemy would love nothing more than to keep our eyes fixed on the potential dangers waiting in the "hills" that surround us, trapping us in a pattern of discouragement. But when we lift our eyes to Jesus, we find that he takes us by the hand and helps us. As Scripture says in Matthew 14:31, "Jesus immediately reached out his hand and took hold of [Peter]," rescuing him from the wind and the waves that threatened to overtake him. This same God is with you and for you, and there are no hills or waves that can overwhelm the steady hand of help he has given you.

When You Feel Forgotten

For I am the LORD your God who
takes hold of your right hand and says to you,
Do not fear; I will help you.

ISAIAH 41:13 NIV

After giving birth to our little girl, Lanie, I was fortunate to have a circle of friends who also had new babies. During those hazy newborn days, we texted each other encouragement through breastfeeding woes and sleepless nights. This connection was the lifeline that kept my head above water through an otherwise wearing, isolating season.

But four months in, Lanie's baby buddies started to leave her behind in one glaring area: sleep. Due to issues related to a tongue tie, Lanie still slept for only two hours at a time. As I began receiving glowing updates from my friends that their babies were now sleeping through the night and eating on a schedule, I wanted to be thrilled for them.

Instead, I sulked. I felt isolated, bitter, and forgotten. Waking up every two hours for months on end while caring for a toddler and a baby takes its toll, and I allowed self-pity to befriend me. It lurked in the shadows, poised to whisper lies as I trudged down the hall for the fourth time in one night to scoop up my crying baby. Self-pity joined me at our messy lunch table where I sat heavy with discouragement from a never-ending morning of picking up sippy cups and shouldering the wearisome monotony of the day. In reality, I fell for that same old lie Eve believed in the garden: God was withholding his goodness from me. Yet the truth was, I was cradling in my arms one of his most beautiful and treasured gifts all along: my precious daughter.

In his mercy, God provided the wisdom I needed to reframe my perspective and pulled me out of a deep emotional pit. He helped me view the constant interruptions of motherhood as merely a "change of assignment." I practiced this new mindset and declared these words aloud, which eventually helped transform my self-pity into a sense of joy and purpose. Whenever I heard my baby cry out while I was preparing a meal, getting dressed, or even sleeping, I would consciously say aloud, "Change of assignment!" and then tend to her needs. This powerful perspective shift helped me to recognize that my role as a mother was not a hindrance or distraction from more important tasks. Rather, it was the exact work God had called me to in this season of life. Through it, he was making me more like him. I was filled with hope as I realized I was not forgotten but had been given a sacred mission by the Lord.

Do you ever feel invisible or forgotten? Are you allowing a circumstance in your life to drag you into the shadows of self-pity? I encourage you to adopt this phrase too—*What is my assignment, Lord? How can I practice joyful obedience in this very moment? How can I serve you by laying down my life for others, as you did for me?* I have continued to ask myself this question for the last ten years because it's a perspective-shaping tool for any season of the Christian life.

Dear sister, if you're in a season that tempts you to feel forgotten by God, be encouraged that these very days of motherhood—as trying as they can be—*are* your current assignment. God has not forgotten you. He sees you with the eyes of a loving Father and has given you this humble, holy work for his glory and for your good.

YOUR SACRED ASSIGNMENT

God does not just give us new assignments to struggle through on our own. He helps us. Here are a few applications from his Word:

- What is your assignment when your toddler has been whining for an hour, and you're ready to snap?

  Remember Proverbs 12:18 and 16:24: "The words of the reckless pierce like swords, but the tongue of the wise brings healing" (NIV); "Gracious words are like a honeycomb, sweetness to the soul and health to the body." Ask the Lord to guard your tongue and fill your mouth with words of love and gentleness, even when you don't feel like offering them.

- What is your assignment when you're feeling overwhelmed or anxious and think you can shoulder heavy burdens on your own?

  Lean on Matthew 11:28: "Come to me, all who labor and are heavy laden, and I will give you rest." Even amid unrelenting needs, he can provide soul rest as we trust in him.

- What is your assignment when you're just plain exhausted from sleepless nights and want to give up?

  Trust the God of Isaiah 40:29: "He gives strength to the weary and increases the power of the weak" (NIV).

- What is your assignment when you feel ashamed for how often you've failed as a mom?

  > Rejoice over Psalm 103:10-12: "He does not deal with us according to our sins, nor repay us according to our iniquities. For as high as the heavens are above the earth, so great is his steadfast love toward those who fear him; as far as the east is from the west, so far does he remove our transgressions from us." Praise him for the unending mercy he has shown us in Christ!

When You're Called to Lay Down Your Own Desires

THE LORD IS YOUR HELP

Love is patient and kind; love does not envy or boast;
it is not arrogant or rude. It does not insist on its own way; it is
not irritable or resentful; it does not rejoice at wrongdoing,
but rejoices with the truth. Love bears all things, believes all things,
hopes all things, endures all things.

1 CORINTHIANS 13:4-7

At a doctor's appointment in late 2020, the nurse glanced at my chart and noticed that I had four young children at home. She snickered, "Oh, that must have been *horrible* living with all of them during the pandemic!" In one sense, her comment wasn't surprising; she was naming a genuine struggle for many moms who had hunkered down at home together for months with few moments of reprieve. But her remark also revealed how our culture views children: it sees them as a burden, a mess, and an unwanted distraction from more important things.

Even as mothers who dearly love our children and confidently say they are anything but a burden, it can sometimes feel like they stand in the way of our plans or comfort. Self-denial doesn't come naturally to anyone, but it is required in motherhood. We sacrifice our time, our bodies, our talents, and so much more for our children. The paradox of motherhood is that it is both remarkably challenging and deeply rewarding. If any other job demanded such unreasonable hours and physical and emotional pain, we would quit on the spot. In weak moments, we are tempted to believe these sacrifices might be a waste. We might even fall for the darkest lie that our children get in the way of "real ministry." But our children are gifts, whether or not they sleep well, eat well, or have easygoing personalities.

The Bible is clear about the value of children and, consequently, the value of mothers. Psalm 127:3 proclaims, "Children are a gift from the LORD; they are a reward from him" (NLT). Our children are clear evidence of God's abundant blessing to us. They are arrows he gives us for a time to love, equip, and then send into the world to boldly display the gospel beyond our home. With our eyes fixed on Christ, we can first savor the great privilege of being loved by God and then extend that love to our children. Whatever the world might say about them, we can assure them of their innate worth in God's eyes and ours.

Have you noticed that Jesus never treated anyone like a burden? Even when he withdrew to desolate places to be away from the crowds and alone with his Father, people would follow him. They hoped he would heal the outcasts of society: the blind, the crippled, the demon-possessed, the mute. Instead of casting them aside like the rest of the world had, Jesus looked on them with eyes of compassion and healed them. They were never burdens to him; they were made in the image of God (Genesis 1:26-27).

Nothing has made me feel so childlike and needy for Jesus as motherhood, yet he has never made me feel like a burden. He has never once dismissed me when I have come to him. He has only loved me, even at my ugliest. And that love has powerfully transformed my heart toward my children.

As you care for your children today, rejoice that you have never once been a burden to God. On the days when your children's needs bring you to the end of your patience, remember his tender patience for you, his daughter. When you sacrifice your desires for your family, lift your eyes to the sacrifice he made for you on the cross. Trust that your hope is secure not because of your faithfulness but because of his.

THREE WORDS THAT HELP CHILDREN FEEL SEEN AND LOVED

When I worked as a nurse, my manager strongly encouraged all staff members to face our patients before leaving the room, ask them if they needed anything else, and say these three words: "I have time." As a nurse juggling heavy patient loads, saying "I have time" didn't always feel realistic or even truthful. But each time those words left my lips, I noticed the patient's countenance soften. Hearing those words helped them to feel seen and cared for.

Those three simple words—*I have time*—are just as powerful in parenting growing kids.

The other day, our 11-year-old son, Liam, planned a five-course Greek meal. He didn't expect us to make it, but when I saw his culinary dreams on paper and knew how much it would mean to him, I said, "Let's do it, buddy! I'll be your sous chef. *I have time*." His eyes lit up with joy. As an aspiring chef, he was thrilled to have the chance to make the meal. I could have spent two hours doing many other things. But getting a front-row seat to my son's passion for cooking, investing in our relationship, and making a precious memory was the best use of time.

"I have time."

Our children need our time. They need us to *make* time to learn about their passions and enter their world. Let your children help you prepare a meal or do a project, even if it takes twice as long. Put your phone in the other room and have an undistracted conversation. When you do, they will know they are anything but a burden—they will feel seen, known, and treasured.

When You Feel Overstimulated and Overwhelmed

THE LORD IS YOUR HELP

When I am overwhelmed,
you alone know the way I should turn.

PSALM 142:3 NLT

With a little one asking for a third snack, *Wild Kratts* playing in the background, and piles of laundry demanding attention, life with children can sometimes feel like sensory overload. Beyond that, my kids' never-ending questions, from "What is the wingspan of the largest flying bird?" to "Why did Grandpa have to die?" often leave me with little time for quiet moments to think.

At the same time, I already anticipate that noise will be the first thing I miss the day our youngest child drives away. I will long to hear the Doxology sung every night at bedtime. I will yearn to listen to my children share their highs and lows around the dinner table. Realizing that this phase of life is fleeting helps me to be grateful to God for the evidence of his answered prayers right here and now. Where there is noise, there is life—and as mothers, we have been given the gift of life.

Jesus understood feeling overwhelmed. During his time on earth, he faced more than just overstimulating noise. Jesus endured formidable opposition, threats from his enemies, and even objections from his followers. He regularly felt sorrow and grief; nothing about his life was quiet or easy.

As we've seen before, Jesus often withdrew from noisy places to pray to his Father (Luke 5:16). If our sinless Savior needed time to be alone with God, how much more do we? Being in God's presence gives us the strength, joy, and endurance we need to face our most overwhelming days.

But we also see Jesus tenderly welcoming noisy children and meeting the needs of the boisterous crowds who followed him (Matthew 15:30). He could have stayed in heaven, enjoying peaceful unity with the Father and the Holy Spirit. But his great love for us compelled him to willingly enter our noise.

How does God's Word speak to us when we are feeling overstimulated and overwhelmed? Philippians 4:4-7 gives us clear instructions: "Rejoice in the Lord always; again I will say, rejoice. Let your reasonableness be known to everyone. The Lord is at hand; do not be anxious about anything, but in everything by prayer and supplication with thanksgiving let your requests be made known to God. And the peace of God, which surpasses all understanding, will guard your hearts and your minds in Christ Jesus."

Let's examine verses 6 and 7, phrase by phrase, and apply these truths to our lives as moms.

Do not be anxious about anything. This command is hard to obey when our children are sick, our bills exceed our paychecks, or we fear the dangers of the world our kids are growing up in. But God repeatedly commands in Scripture, "Do not fear." Our feelings of overwhelm or anxiety can sometimes reveal that we doubt God's care for

us. Or perhaps we are feeling stressed due to an overpacked schedule, and we need to prayerfully consider how we can prioritize what's
important and let go of what's not.

*But in everything by prayer and supplication with thanksgiving let
your requests be made known to God.* God already knows what we need
before we ask, but entrusting our worries to him is powerful for *us*.
He asks us to be prayerful, not anxious, and to transfer our fears from
our weak, burdened shoulders to his strong, capable hands. By thanking him "in everything," we acknowledge that whatever God sends us
is for our ultimate good.

*And the peace of God, which surpasses all understanding, will guard
your hearts and your minds in Christ Jesus.* When we consciously turn
from the overwhelming noise of life to prayer and thanksgiving, God
promises his peace. Even amid the noise of our daily lives, God can
faithfully bring our thoughts back to him and assure us of his unwavering love and sustaining power. When we turn to him, he gives us
peace that defies the noise surrounding us. Picture his peace as a
sentry, guarding the believer's heart and thoughts from anxiety and
despair.

Do you feel overstimulated or overwhelmed? I encourage you
to memorize and meditate on Philippians 4:4-7. Then take a deep
breath, sister. His peace will guard your heart and mind.

When Your Cup Runs Dry

We have this treasure in jars of clay,
to show that the surpassing power
belongs to God and not to us.

2 CORINTHIANS 4:7

We've all seen the T-shirts marketed to moms that say, "All I need is a little coffee and a whole lot of Jesus."

Jesus plus coffee.

Jesus plus wine.

Jesus plus a girls' night out.

Jesus plus eight hours of uninterrupted sleep.

Even well-meaning friends might say, "You can't pour from an empty cup." But in my experience of motherhood, pouring from what feels like an empty cup is a near-daily reality. I often find myself needing to respond with kindness even when I'm sleep-deprived, to comfort a hurting child when I'm hurting too, and to give and give while my own needs are put on the back burner. While I believe rest, boundaries, and even time away to recharge are essential in demanding seasons of motherhood, I have found that my empty cup is the holy place where my great need and God's lavish grace meet. It's where he has repeatedly proven that in my weakness, he is strong.

If we look to Jesus for how he refueled during demanding seasons, we see him retreating from the crowds to a solitary place to pray (Matthew 14:23; Mark 1:35; Luke 5:15-16). Before, during, and after grueling days of ministry, he spent time communing with his Father. Why? Because Jesus was being strengthened and replenished in order to be poured out.

Like Jesus, our own self-care should have the same purpose: strengthening our souls through communion with God so we may serve others. We depend on our Father to care for us so we can care for our families.

What might this look like for a busy mom who is almost always surrounded by the needs of her children? For me, I aim to wake up earlier than my kids to feed my body and my soul. I read or listen to the Bible, and pray for the Lord to sustain me through another day. I use the remainder of that time to do a short workout and prepare breakfast. Depending on the context of your life, your routine will look different—especially if you're not currently sleeping through the night. And that's okay!

Whatever my morning looks like, I expect to feel depleted by the end of the day or even sooner. I have learned firsthand that God cares deeply for those with nothing left to give, and he carries them when they run on empty. There's nothing wrong with indulging in a strong cup of coffee or getting eight rejuvenating hours of sleep—those good gifts can help us move forward with gratitude and joy. But Jesus offers us something far more lasting. He invites us to "come to me, all who labor and are heavy laden, and I will give you rest" (Matthew 11:28). He asks us to cast all our anxiety, all our fear, and all our uncertainty on him because he cares for us (1 Peter 5:7). We no longer need to pursue temporary comforts when Jesus has given us himself.

Let's turn our eyes away from our self-care-obsessed culture and instead lift them to Jesus, who was poured out as an offering for us. Let's shift our perspective from "How can I fill my cup?" to "How will Jesus meet me in this low place when my cup is empty?"

If you need a break, steal away for a moment and look to God's Word for encouragement. If you're not sure where to begin, here are a few Scriptures that have proven life-giving to me on those empty-cup days:

> Isaiah 40:11: "He will tend his flock like a shepherd; he will gather the lambs in his arms; he will carry them in his bosom, and gently lead those that are with young."

> Isaiah 66:13: "As one whom his mother comforts, so I will comfort you; you shall be comforted in Jerusalem."

> Romans 8:38-39: "I am sure that neither death nor life, nor angels nor rulers, nor things present nor things to come, nor powers, nor height nor depth, nor anything else in all creation, will be able to separate us from the love of God in Christ Jesus our Lord."

> 2 Corinthians 12:9-10: "He said to me, 'My grace is sufficient for you, for my power is made perfect in weakness.' Therefore I will boast all the more gladly of my weaknesses, so that the power of Christ may rest upon me. For the sake of Christ, then, I am content with weaknesses, insults, hardships, persecutions, and calamities. For when I am weak, then I am strong.'"

> 1 Peter 5:6-7: "Humble yourselves, therefore, under the mighty hand of God so that at the proper time he may exalt you, casting all your anxieties on him, because he cares for you."

When You've Reached the End of Your Own Strength

THE LORD IS YOUR HELP

He said to me, "My grace is sufficient for you,
for my power is made perfect in weakness."

2 CORINTHIANS 12:9

Some mornings, before I even open my eyes, the voice in my head declares, "I can't." I can't handle one more diaper to change, one more spill to mop up, or one more pitiful attitude (especially my own). Perhaps you've been there too, feeling the weight of the day before it even begins.

After moving from Tennessee to North Carolina as a family of three, our first summer appeared as smooth as the glassy water on Shelley Lake. There were day trips to the coast, sunny picnics at the park, and loads of time with grandparents and cousins.

But alongside those peaceful moments, our daily reality was more like a churning ocean in the middle of a storm. We hadn't anticipated the upheaval of living out of boxes for months or the financial stress that came with purchasing our first home. On top of that, we found ourselves rushing our two-year-old, Liam, to the hospital in the middle of the night when his breathing became labored.

By seven the next morning, we made it home with a sleepy little boy and hungry bellies. My husband, Shawn, whipped up some scrambled eggs, and we stared at each other with bleary eyes. This scary middle-of-the-night hospital run had officially brought us to the end of our own strength.

Shawn flipped open his Bible as we ate and landed on Psalm 91:14-16. "Read this," he said, pushing his Bible across the table toward me. "God sees and cares about what we're going through."

> Because he holds fast to me in love, I will deliver him;
>   I will protect him, because he knows my name.
> When he calls to me, I will answer him;
>   I will be with him in trouble;
>   I will rescue him and honor him.
> With long life I will satisfy him
>   and show him my salvation.

If you are united to Christ by faith, you can personalize these verses and read them aloud to remind yourself that the Lord is your Helper, no matter what you are enduring: "Because (insert your name) holds fast to me in love, I will deliver her; I will protect her, because she knows my name. When she calls to me, I will answer her; I will be with her in trouble; I will rescue her and honor her. With long life I will satisfy her and show her my salvation."

When you meditate on God's Word, you remind yourself who he has promised to be. His Word points you straight to the one who strengthens and upholds your weary, anxious heart. According to his Word, you can trust that his grace is sufficient because his power is made perfect in your weakness (2 Corinthians 12:9). You can cling to the hope that he will strengthen you with power through his Spirit according to the riches of his glory (Ephesians 3:16). Reaching the end of your own strength can become a gift that brings you to your knees before your all-powerful God.

There is a common saying people use in hopes of comforting a discouraged person: "God will never give you more than you can handle." While they mean well, this is not biblical. In fact, God does give us more than we can handle so we ask him for help and lean on his strength, not ours. So the next time you reach the end of your strength and admit, "I can't," let it be an invitation to lift your eyes to the one who can—your all-sufficient Helper.

BOOK RECOMMENDATION

All Who Are Weary: Finding True Rest by Letting Go of the Burdens You Were Never Meant to Carry by Sarah Hauser

PART TWO

The Lord Is Your Provider

My help comes from the LORD, who made heaven and earth.

PSALM 121:2

From where does my help come?" the psalmist asks. He immediately answers his own question by singing in the face of fear: "My help comes from the LORD, who made heaven and earth." This answer reflects his faith that the Creator of the cosmos—a God of boundless power—is able to provide all he needs for his journey.

In the book of Genesis, Abraham and Sarah feared they would never have a child; however, in their old age, God promised that Sarah would indeed have a son. Her response? She did not sing, like the psalmist. Instead, she laughed. Her reproductive years had long passed, and *now* she is to have a child?

But is anything too hard for the Lord? The first cries of baby Isaac—the child God promised to Abraham and Sarah—prove that the answer is no. Despite Sarah's old age and lack of faith, the Lord still fulfilled his promise because his promise was not dependent on her, but on him. And despite Sarah's initial unbelief, God was true to his promise to provide a much-longed-for child. Little did

Sarah know that God was not merely providing for her desire to be a mother: Through Isaac's lineage, Jesus, the long-awaited Messiah, would be born. Through these seemingly impossible circumstances, God was miraculously providing a Savior for Sarah and for the world.

This story reminds me that God's work doesn't hinge on my great faith. Whether I am singing or weeping or doubting or laughing, he has already provided an answer in Jesus, our ultimate Provider. While on earth, Jesus not only provided for physical needs like bread and water, but for spiritual needs, like forgiving sins and casting out demons. Even now, he is our Provider: He provides peace when we're restless, escape when we're facing temptation, and help when we're hurting. He is always doing far more than what we can see on the surface.

When we find ourselves on the verge of laughing in disbelief in the face of God's promises, let's remember his perfect record of faithfulness. Our God has never once failed to keep his promise. Knowing this, we can be confident that he will always care for us.

When You Know You're Not Enough

THE LORD IS YOUR PROVIDER

In Him I have an offering, an altar, a temple, a priest, a sun, a shield, a Savior, a Shepherd, a hiding place, a resting place, food, medicine, riches, honor, in short, everything.

JOHN NEWTON[1]

A quick search for the hashtag #youareenough on Instagram yields more than three million results, which means that you, too, have likely been bombarded by this mantra.

But is it true?

When you're running on a meager three hours of sleep, and your toddler throws a fit, do you find the restraint from within yourself to respond in love? Are you alone enough to supply your needs when bills mount and bank accounts run dry? Can you draw the strength from your own reserves to keep going when life feels like a crucible of stress and disappointment?

In my own experience, motherhood has shattered the illusion that I can summon the strength and goodness my children need from within myself. As much as I strive to be a good mom, there are days I can barely see past my selfish heart to love others well.

Our first son, Liam, was as easygoing as babies come. He ate well, slept soundly, and was generally content. I took pride in my innate mothering skills that had produced such a well-mannered child—until he turned a year old. As he entered the toddler phase, Liam began to show his vibrant, strong-willed colors and boundless energy. He loved to scream happily during story time at the library, pull things from grocery shelves, and run to hide from me when we were in public. He was insatiably curious about the world around him, as toddlers tend to be. Once, he bit into a shiny glass ornament to see how it tasted, sending us straight to the ER.

Parenting Liam as a toddler made me question any notion that I knew what I was doing as a mom. I now realize that my frustrations were ultimately about me, not him. When he blatantly misbehaved, ran off, or was the loudest in the room, I feared it reflected poorly on my parenting.

We will never find all that our kids need within ourselves. Without the Holy Spirit's help, we aren't strong, kind, or patient enough to be good moms for long. We may be able to draw from our natural strengths for a time, but soon, exhaustion will overtake us.

So, where do we find hope?

The New City Catechism Question 1 states it beautifully:

Question: What is our only hope in life and death?

Answer: That we are not our own but belong, body and soul, both in life and death, to God and to our Savior Jesus Christ.[2]

When we take this to heart, we realize that we don't have to find the strength, courage, joy, goodness, or patience within ourselves because we do not belong to ourselves. We belong to the God who owns the cattle on a thousand hills. He knows no lack and willingly provides everything we need. *He* is more than enough. We can lift our eyes to him and say out loud, "Lord, I'm struggling to be patient and kind, and I need your strength to be the mom you have called me to be." As our children hear us cry out to God and see us relying on him, our need can become a gift to them. When we reach the end of our rope and the end of ourselves, we can point them to our mighty God who promises to provide.

In John 15, Jesus describes himself as a vine and those who believe in him as branches depending on that vine for everything they need. If a branch is cut off from the vine, can it still grow? Obviously not. A branch must be connected to the vine to develop and produce fruit. "I am the vine; you are the branches," Jesus says. "Whoever abides in me and I in him, he it is that bears much fruit, for apart from me you can do nothing" (John 15:5). Our Provider supplies for us in ways we could never provide for ourselves. So walk forward in confident dependence on him, freed by the truth that you were never called to be enough.

When You Need to Remember
That God Will Provide

THE LORD IS YOUR PROVIDER

[God] will never cease to help us until we cease to need.
The manna shall fall every morning until we cross the Jordan.

CHARLES H. SPURGEON[1]

George Müller was a faithful believer who dedicated his life to caring for orphaned children in England during the 1800s. He established schools, distributed Bibles, and supported various missionary endeavors. But what set George Müller apart was his unwavering trust in God's provision.

In his journals, he recounted a morning at the orphanage when all the children's plates, cups, and bowls on the tables were empty. The pantry was bare, and there was no money to buy food or milk. As the children stood there, waiting for their morning meal, Mr. Müller prayed aloud, "Dear Father, we thank Thee for what Thou art going to give us to eat." Can you imagine the immense faith it must have required to lift his eyes to God in that moment?

Suddenly, there was a knock at the door. It was the baker. He said, "Mr. Müller, I couldn't sleep last night. Somehow, I felt you didn't have bread for breakfast, and the Lord wanted me to send you some. So I got up at 2:00 a.m. and baked some fresh bread, and have brought it."

After thanking the baker, Mr. Müller heard another knock on the door. It was the milkman, who told him "that his milk cart had broken down right in front of the orphanage, and he would like to give the children his cans of fresh milk so he could empty his wagon and repair it." God had come through miraculously and victoriously.[2]

This story may amaze you, but it might not feel relatable. You may have never stared at a table with empty cups and bowls. Your pantry has bread, your fridge has milk, and your closet is probably stuffed with more clothes than you'll ever be able to wear. While your needs may look different than George Müller's, all of us rely on God's provision. You may need a better paying job or more flexible hours. You might be searching for community or a church family. Or perhaps you need wisdom to navigate a relational conflict or broken friendship. Philippians 4:19 promises that our "God will supply *every need* of yours according to his riches in glory in Christ Jesus" (emphasis added).

The God we serve is the same God who provided enough heaven-sent manna for the Israelites to survive in the wilderness for 40 years. When Adam and Eve sinned and their eyes were opened to the shame of their nakedness, God provided clothes to cover them. And even when we fail him today, God still provides. When Peter denied Jesus three times, Jesus forgave him and still gave him a pastoral role, saying "Feed my sheep" (John 21:17). Seeing how God has cared for his people in the past helps us cling to the promise that he will provide for us now. Even when we don't acknowledge his provision, he still provides: the breath in your lungs, the food in your belly, and the faith to trust him are gifts from his generous hand.

In Matthew 14, Jesus performed a miracle by feeding more than 5,000 hungry mouths with only five loaves of bread and two fish. He said to the boy who brought his small offering the same thing he says to us: *Bring me the little you have, and I will make it enough.* You may feel like you have little to offer your children, let alone the world. But be assured that God's provision extends beyond the physical realm. He provides rest—and isn't that good news for moms (Matthew 11:28)? He provides direction (Proverbs 20:24). He provides escape from the claws of temptation (1 Corinthians 10:13). He blesses us with peace (Romans 5:1; Philippians 4:7). God supplies every ounce of strength and wisdom for us to mother our children for his glory, and he delights to give us exactly what we need exactly when we need it.

When It's Hard to Keep Giving and Serving

THE LORD IS YOUR PROVIDER

Brightly colored sunsets and starry heavens, majestic mountains and the shining seas, and fragrant fields and fresh-cut flowers are not even half as beautiful as a soul who is serving Jesus out of love, through the wear and tear of an ordinary, unpoetic life.

FREDERICK WILLIAM FABER[1]

Recently, I missed church to stay home with my children who were recovering from sickness. I wish I could boast that after a decade of motherhood, I've learned to accept interruptions like these with grace. But I watched the live-streamed service with tears in my eyes, craving fellowship with our church family in a season that felt demanding and lonely. After a long week of restless nights, I was feeling fragile.

But as I sat there, these lyrics from the song "Yet Not I But Through Christ in Me" came through the screen and ministered to my weary heart:

> The night is dark, but I am not forsaken
> For by my side, the Savior he will stay

I labor on in weakness and rejoicing
For in my need, his power is displayed[2]

In the week preceding this particular Sunday morning, sickness had hit our family hard, and all our kids had required breathing treatments at various points. In the midst of this, I contracted the flu while seven months pregnant with our fourth child. I was running a high fever when my husband took our 18-month-old son, Bear, to the doctor. At the doctor's office, Bear took a turn for the worse and had to be rushed by ambulance to the nearest hospital. Within minutes of finding out, I sped to the ER, fever still raging, and ran through the parking lot in my pajamas to reach my son. None of my troubles mattered then—I had to know that Bear would be okay. God was giving me supernatural, incomprehensible strength; his power was evident in my weakness.

As mothers, God gives us miraculous strength to care for others even when we ourselves need care. Are you, too, in the middle of a season of interruptions, sickness, and canceled plans? Do you often feel like you are being asked to keep giving and serving beyond what you can bear? It can be tempting to groan, "I didn't sign up for this," or to give in to exhaustion.

God never promised his children a life void of suffering, trials, or temptations. Jesus assured us, "In this world you will have trouble" (John 16:33 NIV). Sometimes, God allows us to face situations that are too much for us so we learn to cast ourselves fully on him.

Throughout his ministry on earth, Jesus dedicated long, taxing days to serving the needs of those around him. Because Jesus was both fully God and fully man, he experienced every hardship we face (Hebrews 4:15): temptation, hunger, and mental and physical exhaustion. He understands, to an even greater extent than we do, what it means to feel drained and unappreciated. He knows what it's like to live in a body limited by the constraints of a broken world.

While Jesus had the right and authority to demand that others serve him, he instead poured out his life in service to others (Mark 10:45). He showed us the way of giving and serving, even though it cost him his life. When we see our Savior sacrificing his life for ours, it gives us renewed strength to give and serve those around us.

As I finished watching church online that morning, I still had sick kids to care for, but the truth from the hymn stayed with me throughout the day, reminding me that I was, indeed, not forsaken. And remember, dear sister, neither are you.

BOOK RECOMMENDATIONS

Humble Moms: How the Work of Christ Sustains the Work of Motherhood by Kristen Wetherell

Humility: The Journey Toward Holiness by Andrew Murray

When You Feel Lonely

THE LORD IS YOUR PROVIDER

Turn to me and be gracious to me, for I am lonely and afflicted.
The troubles of my heart are enlarged; bring me out of my distresses.
Consider my affliction and my trouble, and forgive all my sins.

PSALM 25:16-18

When I became a mom, I shifted from working full-time as a nurse to staying home with my son and working only a few hours each week. In many ways, spending my days with my precious baby was a dream come true. But the transition from a professional life surrounded by peers to having a newborn as my daily companion felt abrupt and often lonely. Many of my friends were not yet mothers, so our friendships suffered as my schedule now adapted around our new baby's needs. In addition, my husband worked long hours at a demanding job, so our time together was limited to evenings and weekends. Even my relationships at church changed as I rarely got to sit through a full service or attend community group before needing to tend to my son.

You've probably experienced these shifts too. Or perhaps you've felt lonely for other reasons, like a cross-country move, a painful divorce, or the loss of a loved one. In the wake of life changes, we can feel friendless and alone.

If children are living under your roof, it's rare that you are actually alone. You likely spend your days with a baby balanced on your hip, a toddler trailing behind you, or an older child engaged in near-constant conversation. Even so, you may still feel the lonely void of adult relationships because most of your time and attention is rightly devoted to your family.

In Mark 5:25-34, we meet a woman who suffered intense loneliness. This woman had been bleeding for 12 agonizing years and had spent all the money she had in search of medical help, to no avail. Beyond the physical affliction that ravaged her body and mind, she suffered intense social isolation as well. According to Levitical law, excessive blood flow made a woman ceremonially unclean (Leviticus 15:19), and because of this, no one would have wanted to be around her. She couldn't shop at the market or embrace her children, and anything she touched would be deemed unclean. She would have been constantly ashamed.

But when this lonely, hurting woman reached out in defiant faith and touched the edge of Jesus's cloak, she was immediately healed and made clean. In that instant, Jesus not only healed her physical illness but also rescued her from a future of loneliness. He tends to more than just our physical bodies; he also cares for our emotions.

Throughout Scripture, God repeatedly reminds his people of his presence. These reminders can bring comfort to us particularly in lonely seasons. In the Old Testament, he told the Israelites, "I will not leave you or forsake you" (Joshua 1:5), "Fear not, for I am with you" (Isaiah 41:10), and "When you pass through the waters, I will be with you" (Isaiah 43:2). In the New Testament, just before he ascended back to heaven, Jesus promised his followers, "I am with you always, to the end of the age" (Matthew 28:20). The gift of his presence was not only for people in the Bible. It's also for us.

Though no one else may see our lonely hearts, God does. Admit to him how lonely you feel and ask him to remind you of his nearness. Pray that he will provide godly friends who will sharpen and encourage you.

In the meantime, when you think no one else in the world cares for you, remember that Jesus does. Lift your eyes to him and trust that if his Spirit lives within you, you are never truly alone.

ENDURING SEASONS OF LONELINESS

I want to share a few ideas that have helped me navigate periods of loneliness with grace:

1. *Be the friend you hope to have.* Don't wait for someone to reach out to you; be the one who initiates. Invite someone to lunch or a play date at the park. If you want to meet new friends and have the capacity, consider joining a book club or taking a class.

2. *Think outside the box.* If you can't find someone your age and in your stage of life to befriend, what about an older woman who could walk alongside you and be a mentor? Or what about a woman who may be right behind you in your season of motherhood whom you could encourage and disciple?

3. *Say yes.* When we moved from North Carolina to Texas, I decided to say yes to every invitation offered to us during our first year in a new place. Saying yes helped me and our kids form friendships we would never have found otherwise.

4. Most importantly, remember that you have a friend in Jesus and the Holy Spirit dwells within you to give you strength to endure seasons of loneliness, no matter how long they may last.

When Motherhood
Feels Too Hard

THE LORD IS YOUR PROVIDER

Now, O LORD, you are our Father; we are the clay,
and you are our potter; we are all the work of your hand.

ISAIAH 64:8

Have you ever watched a potter working at his wheel? What begins as an inauspicious ball of clay becomes one of the masterpieces that adorns a studio shelf—a vase with intricate latticework, a delicately scalloped bowl, a coffee mug glazed in vibrant colors. Each of these unique creations started as the same thing—a lump of mud. But through the potter's skill and intention, they were transformed into objects of beauty and purpose.

When I took a pottery class at a local community center, I was struck by a crucial part of the process called *wedging*. Before the clay can be shaped into anything useful, the potter must forcefully remove air bubbles by slamming the clay onto the table and casting his full weight onto it again and again. If the clay could feel anything, the force would be painful. But if the clay is to be useful, wedging is necessary. If air bubbles aren't wedged out, the piece will explode when exposed to the high temperatures of the kiln. In the same way, our Potter God uses the trials of motherhood to lovingly wedge us. We may feel pushed and prodded to our limits, but by his grace, he uses these trials to humble, refine, and mold us into his likeness.

For example, patience does not come naturally to me. But after hearing my child call out "Mama?" countless times each day, I have learned to ask the Lord to change *me* instead of bristling in exasperation. I am not, by nature, servant-hearted. I have a tendency to prioritize my own comfort. But motherhood, in its very nature, is others-oriented. Through denying myself for the sake of my children, the Lord has softened me from someone who is easily irritated and wants to pull away into someone who loves to draw near to her family. More than anything else in my life, God has used motherhood as a means of chiseling off my rough edges and making me more like him.

Not only is God shaping us as mothers, but he is also using us to help shape our children. As we teach and nurture them to be salt and light, we participate with the Potter in his work of creating beautiful vessels. As you spend your days with your children and sow seeds of faith in their hearts, you are like a potter—shaping the hearts of the next generation. But it isn't always easy. First Peter 5:8-9 reminds us,

> Be sober-minded; be watchful. Your adversary, the devil, prowls around like a roaring lion, seeking someone to devour. Resist him, firm in your faith, knowing that the same kinds of suffering are being experienced by your brotherhood throughout the world.

Unsurprisingly, the enemy seeks to sabotage God's glorious work in and through us, whether through discouragement, distraction, or lies.

When motherhood feels too difficult, remember that God sees you. He is molding you into a woman of deep inner strength. Not only that, but he invites you to partner with him in shaping your children's lives. This is the very reason we must be rooted in the Word, saturated in prayer, and filled with thankfulness.

At the end of a day when motherhood felt especially hard, I glanced at my nightstand and saw two books: a popular parenting guide and my Bible. As I thought of the wisdom I lacked, I was reminded by the Holy Spirit that God's Word is more valuable than an entire stack of parenting books. The Word of God is alive and active (Hebrews 4:12). His voice is wiser than any advice you might receive from even the most experienced parent. Let's lean on his wisdom, especially on the tough days. God promises to use every difficult circumstance for your good—to transform both you and your children into the masterpieces he has intended.

PROMISES TO CLING TO WHEN MOTHERHOOD FEELS TOO HARD

- God is with you (Joshua 1:9; Psalm 145:18-19).
- He will guide you (Psalm 119:105; James 1:5-6).
- He is always working (John 5:17; Philippians 2:13).
- He hears your prayers (Jeremiah 29:12-13; 1 Peter 3:12).
- He will provide all you need (Psalm 34:10; Psalm 37:25).

PART THREE

The Lord Is the God
Who Sees: *Jehovah El Roi*

He will not let your foot be moved; he who keeps you will not slumber.

PSALM 121:3

In Psalm 121:3, the psalmist affirms God's watchful care over his children. He is a God who guards and keeps them; he never sleeps and never lets them out of his sight.

In the Old Testament, God revealed himself as El Roi—"the God who sees"—to a woman named Hagar. Hagar was an Egyptian servant who worked for Sarah, a woman unable to bear children (see part two for more of Sarah's story). When Sarah doubted that God would provide the child he promised, she took matters into her own hands and asked Hagar to sleep with her husband, Abraham. But when Hagar became pregnant, Sarah mistreated her to the point that Hagar fled into the wilderness in desperation. Despite feeling alone and abandoned, Hagar was not hidden from God's watchful eye, and he sent an angel to comfort her. After this encounter with the Lord, Hagar testified, "You are a God of seeing…Truly here I have seen him who looks after me" (Genesis 16:13).

This story reminds us that even in our lowest moments, when it

feels like no one else sees us, God does. The work of motherhood often goes unseen. You may feel like no one is watching as you lovingly tend to scraped knees and hurt feelings, pack lunches day after day, or fold yet another load of laundry. But your Savior sees every big and small thing you do in secret.

Beyond just seeing, our God attends to us around the clock. He is always vigilant. He is a God who will "instruct you and teach you in the way you should go; [who] will counsel you with [his] eye upon you" (Psalm 32:8). He will not let your foot be moved even an inch off the path he set for you.

Whenever you doubt that God is there, remember Hagar's story. Or when you feel unseen, remember that his eyes roam the earth, looking to strengthen those who are committed to him (2 Chronicles 16:9). He sees you. He knows you. And he has never, for a single moment, taken his eyes off you.

When You Wonder If Your Requests Matter to God

THE LORD IS THE GOD WHO SEES

I love the LORD, because he has heard my voice and
my pleas for mercy. Because he inclined his ear to
me, therefore I will call on him as long as I live.

PSALM 116:1-2

From a reclined table in the dark ultrasound room, I held my husband's hand as we glowed over the sight of our squirmy baby—our first child. We marveled at his perfectly formed head, fluttering heart, and tiny hands opening and closing. Everything seemed flawless to our untrained eyes.

But as the sonographer finished her measurements, she seemed intent on getting a clearer picture of our baby's left foot. At first, I didn't worry. But as the clock ticked on and she asked me to change positions for a better look, fear crept in.

She left the room to consult a radiologist and returned with their joint assessment: the baby's left foot looked turned, like a clubfoot, a condition possibly related to other genetic disorders. We would need to schedule a more in-depth ultrasound and meet with a genetic counselor.

There on the ultrasound table, I silently pleaded in prayer, *Lord, please heal my son. And if not, help me to know that you see us and you care.*

Still, my husband and I left the office feeling deflated. This moment we'd dreamed of—seeing our son for the first time—left us feeling uncertain and scared. On the car ride home, hot tears of disappointment rolled down my face. I fixated on the black-and-white picture of our baby's left foot lying in my lap and allowed my mind to slip into dark territories of fear, pity, and guilt.

Had I done something to cause this?

What if he was never able to play soccer like his daddy did?

What if this turned left foot was the sign of something more serious?

That night, our family and friends hosted a gender reveal party, and I felt guilty for not being more excited. I wanted to be genuinely joyful about our new baby, but all I could see was his turned left foot. In my weaker moments, I wondered if God saw or even cared.

But then something happened that I never could have foreseen.

After the big reveal—"It's a boy!"—a friend's little girl gave us an unexpected gift. I unwrapped a small square box to reveal a cookie cutter in the shape of a tiny left foot. On the card were the words of Psalm 139:14: "I praise you, for I am fearfully and wonderfully made. Wonderful are your works; my soul knows it very well." Only our parents knew about our baby's left foot, so this little girl had no idea of the significance of her gift. But God knew. All day, I had wondered if my inner requests mattered to God. Through something as unexpected as a cookie cutter, he reminded me that he sees and cares and he makes no mistakes—even if it doesn't make any sense to us at the time. In that instant, I felt deeply, irrefutably loved and known by the Lord.

This moment reminded me of Luke 18:1-8, where Jesus tells his followers about a persistent widow who kept asking a judge to hear her case. Finally, the exasperated judge gave her what she wanted just so she would leave him alone.

Jesus uses this story to remind God's children that our heavenly Father is nothing like the judge in the parable. God never grows weary of listening to his children. In fact, Jesus admonished us to keep asking, keep seeking, and keep knocking (Matthew 7:7). By doing so, he affirms that our requests matter to God.

We may not receive immediate, miraculous answers to every longing. He may not reveal that our children are going to be okay, that we're going to get the job, or that he's going to rid our bodies of disease. But Romans 8:28 reminds us that God is always at work, weaving everything together for his glory and our good.

A few weeks after our initial appointment, we found ourselves in another ultrasound room.

"His feet look pretty perfect to me," said the ultrasound tech, this time with a smile as she swiveled the black-and-white screen to face me. I fought back tears. Knowing the deep love a mother has for her child, I believe that we would have been okay even if our son had been born with no feet at all because God would have met us there. In those uncertain weeks, God reminded me that he saw both me and my unborn child, and that he is present in the tiniest details of our lives.

The same Jesus who healed the sick, provided food for the hungry multitudes, and raised the dead to life stands ready to listen to your requests too. Because we belong to God, our requests matter a great deal to him. Bring before him every need you have—great or small.

When You're Angry

THE LORD IS THE GOD WHO SEES

*Know this, my beloved brothers: let every person be
quick to hear, slow to speak, slow to anger; for the anger
of man does not produce the righteousness of God.*

JAMES 1:19-20

Anger.

It's not something we readily confess, but many of us have
discovered this emotion lurking inside, simmering and
often erupting amid the demands of motherhood.

When our first baby, Liam, was just five days old, I was riding tur-
bulent waves of postpartum hormones. Like many brand-new moms,
I hadn't slept, and I was struggling to breastfeed. He screamed as he
tried to latch, both of us desperate for relief. After what felt like hours
of struggle, an unexpected flood of rage pulsed through my veins.
With trembling hands, I set Liam down and screamed into a pillow,
feeling out of control and afraid of myself. I had never experienced
such intense anger as I did that day, and toward a helpless little guy I
loved so much.

After each subsequent child was born and sleepless nights ensued,
my battle with anger reared its ugly head. I cherished each new

precious baby; but even so, many days I was snappy, sharp-tongued, and utterly joyless. I found it impossible to break out of this vicious cycle on my own.

And yet, I was too ashamed to admit this struggle to anyone, even to myself. How could I feel so angry toward these innocent children I adored? In the fog of the newborn days, it was difficult to determine how much of this struggle with anger was due to hormonal imbalances and how much came from deeper places in my soul. I look back and realize now that I could have been helped by a doctor or counselor.

Still, in my desperation and confusion, God was faithful to meet me. "Lord, I don't want to be locked in this pattern," I prayed. "Please, Father, bring joy. Give me self-control. I am helpless without you." Over time, this prayer was answered, often in very practical ways. I learned that if I could prioritize sleep, I would be better prepared to handle my frustration. Going outside to get fresh air, soak up vitamin D, and exercise lifted my mood. I also sought accountability by asking a friend to check in on me. Balancing my blood sugar by cutting out refined sugar and junk food also helped stabilize me. As God guided me toward these practices and my hormones leveled out, my disposition toward my kids gradually changed from bitterness to joy.

As mothers, we set the tone in our homes. Theologian Sinclair Ferguson admonishes parents, "[Children] breathe in the atmosphere we breathe out."[1] None of us wants to create an atmosphere of fear, guilt, or shame. But we don't know how to climb out of this cycle on our own; some of these patterns have deep roots, having been learned from previous generations. With Christ, however, we are never powerless to change because the same power that raised Christ Jesus from the dead is at work in us (Ephesians 1:19-20).

If you're struggling with anger in motherhood, you are not alone.

And if you are in Christ, you are not defined by your anger or by your sin but by Christ's righteousness on your behalf. Lift your eyes to the God who is powerful to bring relief, self-control, and peace. He is able! Beyond all the practical ways you can work toward change, remember that you are loved completely by your Maker. You are loved not because you hold yourself together and are always patient with your children but because he has chosen you to be his daughter before he created the world. He has called you into this sanctifying role of motherhood, and he will carry you.

BATTLING ANGER BIBLICALLY

Here are a few strategies that have helped me to lift my eyes to the Lord in my struggle with anger.

1. *Read or listen to Scripture.* Dwelling on truth, even for five minutes, can have a profound impact. I enjoy listening to an audio Bible while doing the dishes, putting on makeup, or going for a walk. In addition, memorizing Scripture and speaking it aloud is a powerful way to combat sin. I suggest committing one of the following verses to memory, and asking the Lord to bring it to mind when you need it most: Hebrews 4:16; Philippians 4:6-7; James 1:19-20; Proverbs 15:1.

2. *When you feel anger rising, take one physical step back.* Then take a long, deep breath before responding. When I pause, I can assess the state of my own heart. I often realize I am not actually upset with my children, though they might have been the trigger at that moment. Usually, I am anxious, exhausted, or stressed about something outside

their control. Sometimes anger reveals that I'm craving care for places in my own soul. Remember that you are responsible for your actions and emotions, not the person making you angry.

3. *Pray.* Our heavenly Father wants us to come to him with our struggles. He is able to give us self-control (2 Timothy 1:7) and promises never to leave us or forsake us. Journal your prayers to trace the pattern of how God is working in your life.

BOOK RECOMMENDATION

Triggers: Exchanging Parents' Angry Reactions for Gentle Biblical Responses by Amber Lia and Wendy Speake

---

If there comes a point when you do not feel safe around your children, please seek immediate help from someone you trust.

When You Feel Unseen

Your eyes saw my unformed body; all the days ordained for me
were written in your book before one of them came to be.

PSALM 139:16 NIV

On what began as an ordinary Tuesday, my husband, Shawn, took out the trash. But on his walk to the garage, a glass shard protruding from the trash bag cut into his calf muscle and sliced through an artery. He stumbled into the house, bleeding and calling out for help. In God's providence, I was only a few steps away. From my experience as a nurse, I instinctively knew to grab a kitchen towel, tie it like a tourniquet around his leg, and call 911. Shawn lost consciousness, but paramedics arrived within minutes, whisking him away by ambulance to a local hospital for emergency surgery.

A few hours after the accident, I learned that Shawn would ultimately recover. But my relief was short-lived. For the next week, I woke up repeatedly in a cold sweat, sifting through the trauma of that not-so-ordinary Tuesday and allowing my mind to wander to the many *what ifs* still lingering after the incident. What if Shawn had been home alone? What if this day had altered our lives forever?

A dear friend advised me to pray through each distressing image that popped in my mind and to intentionally envision God's watchful presence on the day of the accident. So whenever I recalled those terrifying moments, I trained myself to consciously discern where God was. In doing so, I knew him as the God who Sees. I realized in hindsight that in those initial moments after the accident, God had been there, guiding my hands to stop the bleeding. He was there, enabling paramedics to calmly and skillfully stabilize Shawn. He was there, directing the trauma surgeon to repair Shawn's leg. And in the following days, we experienced God's watchful care through friends who dropped off meals on our front porch, and through our pastor, who humbly scrubbed our garage floor clean of any lingering signs of the accident.

As I relived those moments that initially felt out of control and outside of God's view, I could now see that we were never alone because we serve a God who sees. Truly, the One who protected us that day did not slumber.

But what about all the other days that feel ordinary and wearisome? The work of motherhood often goes unnoticed, and it's easy to believe the lie that even God himself doesn't see or doesn't care what we endure. On days when the emergencies are more like cleaning up accidents on the carpet or removing gum from a child's hair, you might ask, "Do you see this, God? Do you see me? Do I matter?"

As we live out both the big and small cares of motherhood, we can find comfort in the truth I learned through my husband's accident: our God is El Roi, "the God who sees me." He not only sees our loneliness and pain, our long days, our mundane moments, and everything in between—he also understands. Psalm 147:5 (NIV) assures us that "his understanding has no limit." He keeps track of our tears (Psalm 56:8) and is attentive to both good and evil (Proverbs 15:3).

There is nothing that surprises, worries, or befuddles our God. He is never caught off guard, and we can rest confidently in his sovereign control.

I believe we'll look back years from now at our lowest days as moms and confidently declare, "God saw me. He helped me. He didn't leave me to figure out motherhood on my own." The Holy Spirit was always there, watching, guiding, attending to, encouraging, helping, and moving. Though we may not have recognized it then, we will someday acknowledge the unwavering guidance and comfort of God's Spirit on the journey.

When You Need to Remember Who You Are in Christ

THE LORD IS THE GOD WHO SEES

The LORD your God is in your midst, a mighty one who will save; he will rejoice over you with gladness; he will quiet you by his love; he will exult over you with loud singing.

ZEPHANIAH 3:17

D o you remember the life-changing moment you first held your child? The second you locked eyes with that precious, helpless baby, you would have given anything to protect him. You adored each whimper and marveled at every tiny expression. You were swept off your feet by the power of love for a child who could do absolutely nothing in return.

As you ponder that moment, would you believe that the adoration you feel for your child pales in comparison to God's love for you, his beloved daughter?

On the messy and thankless days of motherhood, it's easy to forget that we are loved by the King. It's tempting to feel crushed by criticism and discouraged by defeat rather than to walk confidently in God's love. We might even have moments when we believe God sees us through the same critical lens with which we view ourselves.

In our distorted perception of God's character, we picture him asking us with disdain, "Why was your tone so sharp over something so small? How could you fall for that same temptation? Why can't you just pull it together?" But because of Christ's atoning work on your behalf, which has made you worthy in God's eyes, that isn't his posture toward you at all. No, he is not perpetually disappointed in you but delights in you as his treasured possession (1 Peter 2:9).

That's why we must preach to our hearts that God sees, knows, and loves us unconditionally. And because we are so forgetful, we have to do it again and again. As Tim Keller put it, the gospel is this: "We are more sinful and flawed in ourselves than we ever dared believe, yet at the very same time, we are more loved and accepted in Jesus Christ than we ever dared hope."[1] Dear sister, take comfort in the knowledge that your identity is not defined by what you've accomplished or what you haven't. Your identity is rooted in the love and acceptance of Christ.

It's easy to underestimate the magnitude of motherhood when no one rewards you for your hard work. And yet, even if the world undervalues it, your calling is vital. You are not "just a mom." You are a culture shaper and kingdom builder. The God of the universe chose *you* to teach and nurture the children in your home as an integral part of his glorious plan!

In C.S. Lewis's book *The Lion, the Witch and the Wardrobe*, Edmund Pevensie is the only child in his family who has chosen to go his own way. He has willfully sided with the evil White Witch, only to soon realize he made the wrong choice. After Edmund is rescued, he and Aslan have a long, private talk. While no one knows exactly what is said, Edmund emerges a changed person from that day forward. Later, the White Witch publicly accuses Edmund of being a traitor, which is true. But as she hurls fiery insults at him, Edmund's eyes are fixed on Aslan. He knows that Aslan, not the witch, defines who he truly is.[2]

In the same way, fixing our eyes on Christ helps us grasp our true identity. The enemy can and will hurl insults, some of which may be partly true of us. But when we lift our eyes to Christ, we realize that Christ is already looking at us with the eyes of a loving parent. We know that we are forgiven, accepted, and redeemed on his account.

Dear sister, his love for you is:

exuberant, rejoicing over you with singing (Zephaniah 3:17),

extravagant, giving his only Son for you and not stopping there (Romans 8:32),

tender, mending your broken heart (Psalm 147:3),

long-suffering, even when you're quick to anger (Psalm 86:15),

faithful when you are faithless (2 Timothy 2:13), and

unmerited, given only because of his grace (Ephesians 1:5-6).

When You're Afraid of the Future

I will instruct you and teach you in the way you should go;
I will counsel you with my loving eye on you.

PSALM 32:8 NIV

When I was 19, I spent part of the summer working with indigenous missionaries in the heart of the Amazon jungle of Peru. Each day, we ventured down tributaries of the Amazon River, deep into the rainforest where little to no medical care was available.

One afternoon, our jungle pastor, Jorge, received news of an 11-year-old boy in another village who urgently needed medication we had. Without it, he would die. Jorge invited me to accompany him and his team to deliver the medicine, and we quickly hopped into a motorized canoe. The trip was expected to take around two hours, and Jorge asked if I wanted to steer the boat. I happily obliged.

As the sun set, a thick darkness enveloped the landscape, leaving only the silhouette of the jungle against the horizon. Despite being at the helm, I was completely dependent on Pastor Jorge's expertise to navigate the twists and turns of the Amazon River. He was intimately familiar with these waters, and his instructions were my only hope to avoid the hidden dangers of rocks and branches lurking beneath the water's surface.

At one point, it appeared that we were headed full speed toward the trees. To my right, a wider path through the muddy water seemed like a much safer route. Silently questioning Jorge's instructions, I deviated a little to the right, hoping Jorge wouldn't notice. But each time I did, Jorge's soft, patient voice would guide me back, *"A la izquierda, hija"* ("To the left, daughter"). With sweaty palms and clenched teeth, I battled my own inclinations, forcing myself to trust Jorge's guidance and pull left again and again, despite the overwhelming urge to veer right.

I continued to steer nervously as he instructed, when suddenly I spotted a small inlet on the horizon. I slowed the boat as we made our way into the clear, dark waters that had been hiding from view. We had safely reached our destination.

As a mother, I have often felt like that 19-year-old version of myself on the Amazon River, unable to see what's ahead. The path can feel treacherous and out of control, like steering a speeding boat toward land. Many of my fears stem from the unknown, from what I can't see. When I lose sight of the truth that God is fully aware and in control of the course of my life and my children's lives, I am consumed by the uncertainty of the future. I worry that my kids will make poor decisions that yield serious consequences. I dread the possibility that we might become sick or be involved in an accident. I fear that parenting teenagers will be much harder than parenting toddlers, and I will fail as a mom.

But God, in his wisdom, has not given us eyes to see the future. He simply gives us the present and asks us to trust him, moment by moment. As Elisabeth Elliot once wrote, "Today is mine. Tomorrow is none of my business. If I peer anxiously into the fog of the future,

I will strain my spiritual eyes so that I will not see clearly what is required of me now."[1] Jesus sits with us in the boat—able to see the past, present, and future—and guides us patiently, saying, "Stay on *my* course, daughter. You can trust me. My good plan is to give you hope and a future." He knows exactly where we're headed, and with the Spirit as our compass, there is nothing to fear.

When you're afraid of the unknowns of the future, trust that your Jehovah El Roi—the God who sees—won't even let a sparrow fall apart from his will. How much more does he care for you? You may not know exactly what your future holds, but you can trust that God himself is already present there, working all things for your good and for his glory. As believers, we are never really lost on the waters. He is always gently guiding us, whether we perceive it or not.

PART FOUR

The Lord Is Your Protector

Behold, he who keeps Israel will neither slumber nor sleep.

PSALM 121:4

As mothers, our instinct to protect our children is innate. Yet there are times when we, the protectors, also need protection. Like a mama bear seeks refuge from storms, we too need protection from the external world, but also from the internal battles that rage within our minds. But where can we find this kind of protection?

Psalm 121:4 serves as a comforting reminder that our sovereign God is ever vigilant over his people. Unlike us, he never grows weary or distracted. His protection is not sporadic, but a constant, unwavering presence in our lives. He is always ready to intervene with his mighty power.

In his beautiful priestly prayer for us, Jesus said, "While I was with them, I kept them in your name, which you have given me.

I have guarded them, and not one of them has been lost" (John 17:12). The night he prayed that prayer was the same night that he was betrayed. In the garden, Jesus neither slumbered nor slept when our salvation hung in the balance. He stayed awake all night, laboring in prayer about his impending death, which would provide the ultimate, eternal protection for his people. With one mighty blow, Christ's death paid the penalty for our sin, broke Satan's hold, and defeated death's victory over us.

Even when you walk through valleys, you can be confident that "he who keeps Israel will neither slumber nor sleep." Just as God protected and guided his chosen people, he also protects and guides each one of us. You are in his perfect care and under his sovereign protection.

When You Cannot Sleep
Because of Worry

THE LORD IS YOUR PROTECTOR

*In peace I will both lie down and sleep; for you
alone, O Lord, make me dwell in safety.*

PSALM 4:8

One brisk autumn afternoon, I took our two- and four-year-old on a walk to the park. Liam, our oldest, had recently learned to stop at cross streets on his bicycle, so I let him ride a few dozen feet ahead.

I watched as Liam made a sharp left turn into the park. But as I rounded the corner, expecting to see him, all I saw was his bike lying in the middle of the sidewalk. My heart stopped as I frantically searched for my son; there was no sign of him in any direction.

"Liam?" I called, expecting an immediate response. Silence.

"LIIIAAAAMMMM!" I yelled, a primal cry from a mom who needed to find her boy. A woman wearing headphones jogged past, but no one else was in sight. My throat tightened; the world around me blurred.

I screamed once more—a sound Liam would surely hear if he were anywhere close—and suddenly, I heard a familiar giggle from the bushes. "Come get me, Mommy!" Pushing aside a branch, I saw his smiling eyes. "I was jus' hiding from you!"

That episode stayed with me for weeks. It robbed me of sleep, knowing our day could have turned out differently. I took my eyes off my son for ten seconds, and within moments, he was gone.

Even the most attentive mothers cannot watch their children every minute of the day. We have limits. We need to do the dishes or care for another child, and at the end of the day, we need to close our eyes and rest! It's how we were created, and how we spend a third of our lives. Our need for rest is a humbling reminder of our human frailty, isn't it?

Our heavenly Father is wonderfully *unlike* us in this way: he never sleeps. He never dozes off, and he doesn't need a power nap before attending to our needs. No, he's awake and available every second of every day, his eyes running "to and fro throughout the whole earth, to give strong support to those whose heart is blameless toward him" (2 Chronicles 16:9).

Because our God took on flesh and became a real human being, Jesus *did* need sleep, though he never lost his sovereign control over the universe. In Matthew 8:23-27, Jesus is on a boat with his disciples in the middle of the Sea of Galilee when a storm suddenly arises and grips even the most experienced fishermen with fear. The boat is tossed about, water pours in, and the disciples are certain they will perish. But while the storm thrashes the boat, Jesus remains sound asleep. In their terror, the disciples wake Jesus, and he rebukes the wind and the waves. Immediately, the storm obeys and stops.

Jesus turns to his disciples and asks, "Why are you afraid, O you of little faith?" (Matthew 8:26). This is a perplexing response, especially considering the disciples had brought their fear to the right place—to Jesus. At the very least, they had enough faith to know who to ask for help. But as preacher Matthew Henry clarifies for us, "He does not chide [the disciples] for disturbing him with their prayers, but for disturbing themselves with their fears."[1]

Like the disciples, we are often disturbed by our fears. Worries wreck our peace in the middle of the day or night and expose areas of our hearts that don't fully trust God. They might even reveal a false belief that surely God has fallen asleep or turned his back on us.

In the depth of night, when anxiety, guilt, frustration, and despair steal your much-needed sleep, do you believe God is your Protector? Can you trust in his sovereignty over all? Jesus understands the exhausting nature of stress and fear. He knows how anxiety can rob us of peace. That's why he promises to keep and protect us, even in our most vulnerable state—while we sleep.

When you cannot sleep because of worry, remember that God is always awake. His loving eye is constantly upon you. And even when you cannot be there for your children, he is there. He is, in every way at every moment, upholding the universe by the word of his power (Hebrews 1:3). As you lift your eyes to him, you can rest in the knowledge that whether you are asleep or awake, your loving Protector watches over you and your children.

When You Feel Criticized

THE LORD IS YOUR PROTECTOR

There is therefore now no condemnation for those who are in Christ Jesus. For the law of the Spirit of life has set you free in Christ Jesus from the law of sin and death.

ROMANS 8:1-2

Moms are no strangers to criticism about their parenting choices. Even among mothers who are good friends, we all make tough parenting decisions that someone, somewhere, will disagree with, whether it's about school choice, screen time, or discipline methods. Inevitably, someone will misunderstand, judge, or insult us.

When our first baby was six weeks old, we nervously returned to church for the first time as a family of three. Along with an overpacked diaper bag, we carried high hopes that our son's newborn immune system could handle crowds. Halfway through the service, he needed to be fed, so I carried him to the nursing mothers' room, where I found a few ladies feeding their babies in a circle of rocking chairs.

"I would *never* do anything but cloth diaper my babies," one woman was saying. "What a waste. It's terrible for their skin to be up

96 LIFT YOUR EYES

against all those toxins." She went on to describe her plans to nurse her children until age three, to opt out of all ultrasounds, and to have a home birth for her next child with only a doula present. There was nothing wrong with her opinions, but her tone made me feel deeply self-conscious.

I ducked into the corner of the room to change Liam's disposable diaper, hoping her eyes wouldn't wander to me. As I returned to join the rocking chair circle, I grabbed another wet wipe from my bag to wipe his drippy nose.

"*Oh!* I wouldn't touch his face with that," she interjected.

I looked up, stunned that she was talking to me. I had felt invisible up to this point, with hardly a glance in my direction from anyone since I walked in.

"Here, let me grab you a Boogie Wipe," she chided. "It's organic—so much better for his newborn skin."

My face heated up in shame as I accepted the wipe. I felt like crawling behind the chair with my baby to shield us from this intensely uncomfortable moment. In a perfect storm of postpartum hormones and sheer exhaustion, I didn't need a different wipe for my baby—I needed grace.

We all strive to be the best mothers we can be, and when someone doubts or directly discourages our decisions, it can rattle us. In those moments, we can remember how Jesus always remained steady in his calling, even when criticized. As Peter, an eyewitness, recounted, "When they hurled their insults at him, he did not retaliate; when he suffered, he made no threats. Instead, he entrusted himself to him who judges justly" (1 Peter 2:23 NIV). Although we may need to set boundaries in some situations or conversations, we all must entrust ourselves—and our parenting decisions—to God.

In John 8, we see a woman being viciously humiliated, and not just over a difference of parenting opinions. After being caught in the act of adultery, she was brought before religious authorities who shamed her and demanded that she be stoned for her sin. We can't hear the crowd's jeering, but we can imagine the venom they spewed. The scribes and the Pharisees attempted to trap Jesus and wanted him to stone her, in alignment with the Law of Moses. But Jesus said to them, "Let him who is without sin among you be the first to throw a stone at her" (John 8:7).

Stumped by Jesus's request, the religious leaders began to walk away, leaving Jesus alone with this woman. Then, Jesus asked her if anyone accused her, and she said no. Jesus said, "Neither do I condemn you; go, and from now on sin no more" (John 8:10-11).

If you belong to Christ, it is crucial to remember how *he* defines you. Even if you have failed, he does not shame you. Instead, he gently lifts your eyes to him and says five powerful words: "Neither do I condemn you."

The next time you feel attacked or belittled, whether by another person or by the critical voice in your head, remember that you are not defined by

your lost temper,

your pant size,

that missed deadline,

your child's behavior,

a burned dinner,

a blown budget,

what another mom said behind your back, or

even a past sin you're holding onto.

If you are in Christ, you are

chosen,

adopted,

redeemed,
forgiven,
righteous, and
deeply, unconditionally loved.
And *he* has the final word.

When You're Tempted to Speak Harshly to Your Children

THE LORD IS YOUR PROTECTOR

Death and life are in the power of the tongue.

PROVERBS 18:21

When I was in seventh grade, I vividly remember the day all the girls were summoned to meet with the school counselor. We were nervous. What had we done wrong? The counselor sat us down and calmly told us she had overheard some backbiting and gossip among us. Then, she taught us a phrase she hoped we would remember before saying anything: "Is it true? Is it kind? Is it necessary? If it's not all three, then it shouldn't be said." It's been over 20 years since that day, but I've held tightly (though imperfectly) to that phrase.

Is it true?

Is it kind?

Is it necessary?

Wouldn't these three simple filters make a world of difference for us as moms? The words we speak to our children carry enormous weight. They can inspire faith or incite fear. They hold the power to bless or curse. If children are fed a steady diet of "What were you thinking?" or "Haven't we been over this before?" or perhaps even harsher phrases, those words can become a child's inner voice. It doesn't take long for them to believe those words and feel like there is something wrong with them.

God cares how we communicate with our children. They are *his* children, after all, and he has given us the awesome responsibility of caring for his little ones. The words we speak to them express how we value—or don't value—them as God's image bearers.

But moms are God's children too. He parents us as we parent them. The more we get to know God's character by reading his Word and spending time in prayer, the closer we can follow his example and model his life-giving parenting to our children. Even when we fail miserably, he shows us unmerited compassion and kindness. His ultimate desire is always for our good, and his discipline is fueled by love.

One of the ways God parents us is by protecting us from being wounded or from wounding others. As moms, we know that the protection we often need is from ourselves—protection that keeps us from spewing words that hurt. When you feel tempted to speak harshly to your children, stop and remember that the Lord is your Protector. James tells us that "no human being can tame the tongue" (James 3:8). But we don't have to try in our own strength, because we have a generous Father who longs to help us in our weakness. As we lean on him, the Holy Spirit gives us the power to control our tongues, even when it would be much easier to be careless with our words. Because God neither slumbers nor sleeps, he is always awake and ready to guard you against evil, even the evil of your flesh that would tear your children down.

A few months ago, I noticed that my automatic response to my children's persistent "Mama! Mama!" was a sharp and exasperated, "What?!" I began to feel convicted about how frustrated and impatient I sounded toward them, and I prayed for God to change me. In his kindness, he prompted me to pause before I spoke and alter my response from "What?" to "Yes, love?" And do you know what happened? Not only did my tone change—it's nearly impossible to ask "Yes, love?" with anger in your voice—but my heart changed too. By God's grace, my former impatience nearly disappeared and was replaced with tenderness and joy. God worked through this tiny new habit to help me be more gentle and loving toward my children. I pray your heart will soften as you remember God's gracious words to you, allowing you to offer words of grace to your children.

SPEAKING LOVE AND HOPE OVER OUR CHILDREN

As we seek to raise children who think rightly about themselves and about God, I want to share a few biblically rooted blessings you can adopt and speak over your children. These are simple ways to remind them of God's power, wisdom, and goodness and to send them out into the world with confidence that they are secure in his love. When the enemy tempts your children to believe lies, I pray these words of truth will ring louder.

- No matter what, you are loved. Nothing you can do will ever change that (Romans 8:38-39).
- You will never be alone (Matthew 28:20).
- We can do hard things because God is with us (Deuteronomy 31:6).
- God is for you, and he's more powerful than your fears (Psalm 118).

- You are a precious gift from God (Psalm 127:3).
- Let's trust God with that (worry/decision). He'll show us the way (Proverbs 3:5-6).

BOOK RECOMMENDATION

Giving Your Words: The Lifegiving Power of a Verbal Home for Family Faith Formation by Sally and Clay Clarkson

When You Need to Remember That God Is for You

THE LORD IS YOUR PROTECTOR

Out of my distress I called on the LORD; the LORD answered me and set me free. The LORD is on my side; I will not fear. What can man do to me?

PSALM 118:5-6

For six days, I found myself in the most unexpected place: a jury box.

When I reported to the Wake County Justice Center for jury duty—a pregnant mom with three young children at home—I thought my chances of sitting in a trial were slim. But to my bewilderment, I passed every round of selection and was chosen as a juror.

For the next six days, I listened to the testimony of a young girl who had been robbed of her childhood. I heard statements from therapists, social workers, pediatricians, and police detectives. The trial felt emotionally draining and agonizingly slow, nothing like the courtroom dramas on television that cross-examine a witness for 30 minutes and swiftly deliver a verdict.

After all witnesses were presented, the jury was sent to deliberate.

It was apparent that we agreed: the defendant was guilty on every count. As the judge delivered our verdict, I watched the unmoving expression on the defendant's face as each of the five "guilty" verdicts was read. Our decision had sealed a man's fate: in this case, 40 years in prison. Even though the man *was* guilty and deserved this just punishment, the weight of that decision made my knees buckle.

As I walked away from the courthouse after six draining days, I didn't expect this experience to make an aspect of God's character more real to me. But the hours spent in that courtroom gave me a deeper understanding of the concept of substitutionary atonement. It made me contemplate how for believers, Jesus stepped in, took our place, and embraced the full weight of the punishment we deserved when he died on the cross.

Picture this: you're sitting in the defendant's seat in a courtroom, and the judge announces the verdict: "Guilty, guilty, guilty on every count." This is the undeniable verdict for us in our sins. You sit there, heart pounding. You know you deserve the consequences that are coming. But suddenly, the side door of the courtroom opens, and Jesus himself walks in and sits in your place. To your astonishment, the judge starts speaking to Jesus as if he were you and sentences *him* with your punishment. In return, you are given Jesus's perfect record of obedience and dismissed from the courtroom stunned, indebted to and utterly amazed at Jesus, your Savior.

This is your story if you believe in Christ and have personally accepted him as your Savior. You have been justified by faith, declared righteous before a holy God (Romans 5:1)! Your standing before God is not based on the good things you've done. It is based on what Jesus has already accomplished by living the perfect life and dying in your place. What overwhelmingly good news! It is a declaration of pardon and acceptance.

On an average day of motherhood, it is easy to forget that Jesus is for you and is, even now, seated triumphantly at the right hand of God, interceding on your behalf (Romans 8:34). Instead, the needs right in front of you take center stage: the toddler at your feet, the mounting to-do list, the sense of inadequacy after a day that seems wasted. But none of it is wasted. God is actively present, protecting, guarding, and keeping you. There are no average days in God's eyes. They are all precious and deeply meaningful to him, because *you* are precious and deeply meaningful to him.

Considering this reality gives us the emotional wealth to face all of life with deep-seated joy. We can selflessly love others—our spouses, our children, our friends, and even our enemies—when we know how lavishly loved and forgiven we are.

Do you believe God is for you?

When You Battle Discontentment

THE LORD IS YOUR PROTECTOR

I have learned in whatever situation I am to be content. I
know how to be brought low, and I know how to abound.
In any and every circumstance, I have learned the secret
of facing plenty and hunger, abundance and need. I
can do all things through him who strengthens me.

PHILIPPIANS 4:11-13

W ho among us has not longed for a different season of life or motherhood? Before you became a parent, perhaps you had more money or freedom, and life was simpler. Now, you are tethered to the needs of your children throughout the day and often through the night. Perhaps you catch yourself dreaming about a future where your children are grown and you are no longer needed quite as much. Maybe you wish you were done with potty training, or you could return to a career you love. Maybe you just wish you had time to take a nap!

Just after our second child was born, our family was living on a single income—my husband's meager ministry salary—and it became clear this arrangement wouldn't be enough to meet our needs. We decided I would go back to work as a nurse. Within weeks, my life shifted from being at home all the time with my kids to working full-time hours away from them. I went from seeing Shawn on evenings and weekends to only catching a glimpse of his silhouette as I tiptoed into our room past midnight after a long shift at the hospital. While I knew this season wouldn't last forever, I battled feelings of resentment since being away for so many hours meant missing much of my daughter's first year of life. I was working myself to the bone both at home and at work, and in both places, I felt like I was failing.

During this season, I needed to cling to Paul's words to the Philippians: "In any and every circumstance, I have learned the secret of facing plenty and hunger, abundance and need. I can do all things through him who strengthens me" (Philippians 4:12-13). As he wrote these words, Paul was imprisoned in Rome. He had previously traveled all over the continent of Asia preaching the good news. Suddenly his ministry was seemingly brought to a halt as he was put in chains. But even within the confines of a less-than-ideal circumstance, Paul continued to faithfully minister because he knew who was in control. Paul's resolve to choose contentment with the strength of Christ allows us to have his writings, which have spurred Christians on for centuries.

In his letter to Timothy, Paul wrote that "godliness with contentment is great gain" (1 Timothy 6:6). But what exactly do we gain by choosing contentment? We gain peace when we trust that God knows what he's doing. We gain joy when we savor the good gifts he has given us. We can grow, regardless of our circumstances, because we are confident that he has placed us right here, right now, for a purpose. Missionary Jim Elliot wrote in his journal, "Wherever you are, be *all* there. Live to the hilt every situation you believe to be the will of God."[1] As a mother, this exact season with your unique children and circumstances *is* God's perfect will for your life.

One practical way I combat discontentment is by leaning in, a practice that helps me focus on the gifts that God has placed right in my lap. It sometimes looks like this: When the kids misbehave or overreact and you're inclined to push them away, *lean in*. Scoop them up and look into their eyes to discern the real problem. When the house is a disaster and you're tempted to escape into the social media abyss, *lean in*. Put the phone away, turn on happy music, and get to work. Whether comforting a child, caring for your home, or tending to the work and people he has put in front of you, let your intentional presence be an offering of worship to the Lord. When we choose to be fully present, we reflect God's promise of his presence, which is one of his greatest gifts.

What is robbing you of contentment today? Is it your dated home decor, the lack of romance in your marriage, or an illness God has allowed? How could trusting in God's goodness shift the posture of your heart? What might he be protecting you from?

Pray with me: *Lord, protect us from the allure of what we do not have and do not need. Help us rest in you and the good gifts you have given.*

BATTLING DISCONTENTMENT THROUGH STORIES OF THE SAINTS

One way I've learned to combat discontentment is to read the biographies of courageous Christians who have learned that even in the face of formidable challenges, God is enough. Their true stories put my problems in perspective. Here are a few I recommend:

God's Smuggler by Brother Andrew, with John and Elizabeth Sherrill

Heavenly Man by Brother Yun

A Chance to Die: The Life and Death of Amy Carmichael by Elisabeth Elliot

Shadow of the Almighty: The Life and Testimony of Jim Elliot by Elisabeth Elliot

Bonhoeffer: Pastor, Martyr, Prophet, Spy by Eric Metaxas

The Insanity of God: A True Story of Faith Resurrected by Nik Ripken

Evidence Not Seen: A Woman's Miraculous Faith in the Jungles of World War II by Darlene Deibler Rose

The Hiding Place by Corrie Ten Boom, with John and Elizabeth Sherrill

PART FIVE

The Lord Is Your Keeper

The LORD is your keeper; the LORD is your shade on your right hand.

PSALM 121:5

God keeps us as a rich man keeps his treasures,
as a captain keeps a city with a garrison,
as a royal guard keeps his monarch's head.

CHARLES H. SPURGEON[1]

I f there is one thing the psalmist longs to impart, it's this: the Lord is your Keeper. The original Hebrew text of Psalm 121 includes the word *shamar* ("to keep") six times in just five verses. Though some English translations use words like *guard*, *watch*, or *preserve*, the original audience would have understood that the main idea of this psalm is "the Lord who keeps." In Genesis 2:15, the same Hebrew word is used to describe a gardener tending to his garden: watering, pruning, and cultivating with careful attention. The focus is on God's watchful eye on us rather than his lookout for potential enemies. It implies his nearness, like a mother staying close to her child, guiding and protecting them as they learn to walk.

As Jewish pilgrims made their way down the Jordan Valley toward Jerusalem, they faced intense sunlight. Because of this, they would have looked for any kind of shade, whether from trees or hills, to comfort and protect them from the scorching heat. Just as shade was a tangible comfort to them, the psalmist says that the Lord *is* our shade, providing believers with comfort and relief on our journeys.

Your God is your ever-present companion, walking alongside you every step of the way. Because he is your Keeper, he will not lose you. He will not let you wander off into foolishness or sin for long because you are too precious to him. The Lord is your Keeper and your shade, gently tending to you and protecting you from the harsh rays of life.

When You Wonder If You're Making a Difference

THE LORD IS YOUR KEEPER

Let us not grow weary of doing good,
for in due season we will reap, if we do not give up.

GALATIANS 6:9

Many days, being a mother does not feel rewarding or heroic. Perhaps you are in a phase where your days end with dried applesauce on your shirt, a sippy cup leaking under the couch, and dark circles under your eyes. Parenting children of any age stretches your energy and patience to their limits, and often, you have little to show for your hard work. You may wonder if what you're doing is even making a difference.

More than a decade into motherhood, I have learned that our daily choices eventually become habits, and these habits shape our legacy. Fifty years from now, when my children think of me, will they recall seeing me hunched over my phone? Or will they remember my eyes, fully engaged and eager to hear what they have to say? Will they recall my negative, complaining attitude? Will they remember me reading my Bible and consistently opening our doors to people in need? Taking the longer view of motherhood reminds me to reorient my perspective and approach my days with intentionality.

When our oldest son was five years old, I spotted him in our back-yard chatting with our neighbor's young daughter. She was part of a ref-ugee family that had recently emigrated from their war-torn country. Liam and this little girl talked happily as I watched from the window.

When Liam came inside, I asked him what he had been chatting about. He beamed, "Oh, I was just telling her about Jesus and how he died for her sins. I asked her if she knew him." He went on to tell me that he wanted to pray that she and her family would come to know Jesus.

As I stood at my kitchen sink, it struck me once again that my hus-band and I have planted tiny seeds of faith. Others have watered them. *But God*—my two favorite words in all of Scripture—makes them flourish and grow. Even as I strive to establish habits, rhythms, and an atmosphere that will cultivate godly character, ultimately "salvation belongs to the LORD" (Psalm 3:8). I could take no credit for my child's desire to tell others about Jesus. We had only had a few conversations about evangelism, as I had reservations about my five-year-old's capac-ity for comprehension. But God was already at work in his heart, and I witnessed the fruit that he alone was producing in my son.

What does this mean for us as moms? It means that God is not only *our* Keeper but also the faithful Keeper of our children. The very best thing we can do as we walk this journey of motherhood is to be firmly rooted in God's Word, faithful in prayer, and attentive to his voice. Family discipleship is like gardening. We sow seeds of truth in our chil-dren's hearts and wait patiently for God to bear fruit in them. Because it is ultimately the Spirit's work to save and sanctify our children, we can take a deep sigh of relief when we understand we have a Keeper who shepherds our tiny disciples more perfectly than we ever could.

When the Days Feel Mundane

THE LORD IS YOUR KEEPER

*You are as much serving God in looking after your own children,
and training them up in God's fear, and minding the house, and
making your household a church for God, as you would be if you
had been called to lead an army to battle for the Lord of hosts.*

CHARLES H. SPURGEON[1]

M others often think of their daily work as ordinary, mundane, or monotonous. I get it. It's monotonous to wash the same dishes three times a day and sweep up the same crumbs again and again. The repetitiveness of making beds, vacuuming the carpet, and even helping with homework can feel never-ending. Whether you stay at home with your children or have a job outside your home, certain aspects of managing a family and a household can feel tiresome and even trivial, and it's tempting to grumble.

But what if we changed how we perceive the tasks we consider ordinary, mundane, and monotonous and instead saw them as faithful? What if we dedicated every part of the work of motherhood to Christ and allowed him to give it value? When we offer our cooking to the Lord, he helps us see that there is nothing ordinary about nourishing our growing families with well-prepared meals. There is nothing mundane about patiently teaching our children to read and opening their eyes to the wonders of the world. As moms who manage our busy homes, we are privileged to continue God's work of creating order out of chaos. Our faithfulness in even the smallest tasks can give our children a glimpse of the beauty that awaits us in our eternal home.

God's economy is vastly different from ours. What may feel like an unproductive season at home with your children may be your most fruitful years on earth for furthering his kingdom. Your role as a parent and homemaker extends beyond mopping floors and wiping sticky faces. You are investing deeply in your children's souls by laying down your time, energy, and resources for their growth and well-being, just as Jesus did for us. This kind of selfless love defines us as believers and sets us apart from the world. First John 3:16 declares, "This is how we know what love is: Jesus Christ laid down his life for us. And we ought to lay down our lives for our brothers and sisters" (NIV).

When I worked as a nurse, I once cared for a patient who was in the final stages of liver failure. His wife told me, "My favorite nail lady is coming by the hospital to give my husband a manicure and pedicure. It's something that gives him a lot of comfort." That afternoon, I watched from the hall as the manicurist lovingly crouched over a jaundiced, dying man, tending to him with great compassion. As I observed her, I thought of mothers. You aren't often recognized or rewarded for your hard work, but your faithfulness in even the smallest tasks has profound dignity. As you humbly serve your family and reflect Christ, you are lifting the gaze of your children to the King.

Jesus said our sacrifice is like a seed that will produce fruit that we

WHEN THE DAYS FEEL MUNDANE   119

cannot yet see (John 12:23-26). Unless a seed is buried in the soil, it is fruitless. But when it is planted, it produces flowers, trees, and life. In the same way, the days that seem mundane can feel like seeds of sacrifice—like a death of sorts. But what a worthy offering to spend our lives sowing seeds that will produce eternal fruit in the hearts of our children!

Allow the Lord to tend to you as you tend to your children. He is your Keeper, even as you are theirs.

BOOK RECOMMENDATION

Treasuring Christ When Your Hands Are Full: Gospel Meditations for Busy Moms by Gloria Furman

When You Feel Ashamed for How You've Failed as a Mom

THE LORD IS YOUR KEEPER

He does not deal with us according to our sins, nor repay us according to our iniquities. For as high as the heavens are above the earth, so great is his steadfast love toward those who fear him; as far as the east is from the west, so far does he remove our transgressions from us.

PSALM 103:10-12

As much as I adore my children, I sometimes fail them. I run out of patience, lose my temper, and say things I immediately regret. I may discipline them in anger or neglect to discipline them at all. Apart from the leading of the Holy Spirit, I cannot parent in accordance with God's good wisdom.

One sunny spring day, the bickering in our house had reached a record high, and I felt my frustration about to bubble over. So I sent the kids outside to play in the backyard, hoping it would calm us all. Our windows were wide open, allowing a warm southern breeze to blow through the house, and I retreated to our bedroom for a moment of peace. But in less than a minute, my kids appeared, screeching and squabbling on the other side of the open bedroom window. I had had enough. I lunged toward the window, slamming it shut. The windowpane immediately shattered under my force.

My children shrank back, stunned by what had just happened. I fell to my knees, pulling glass shards from the carpet and feeling the sting of my inadequacy and lack of self-control. Then, filled with remorse, I walked outside to mend the damage I had caused in our relationship. Scattered around me was the undeniable evidence of my brokenness as a mom.

Perhaps you turned to this devotion because you too feel the weight of failure today. Maybe you're battling relentless accusations from the enemy who constantly reminds you of your faults. His words are heavy with shame. While we should acknowledge the weight of our roles in our children's lives and the way our sin impacts them, God doesn't want us to be crushed under it. He offers us mercy and grace in our time of need (Hebrews 4:16).

In John Bunyan's timeless allegory *The Pilgrim's Progress*, the main character, Christian, carries a heavy burden on his back that represents his sin. But at the pivotal moment when he reaches the foot of the cross, the burden falls off his back and tumbles down the hill, never to be seen again.[1] This moving metaphor reminds us that we, like Christian, have been forgiven of our sins by Christ once and for all (Hebrews 10:14). No sin you are carrying is beyond his forgiveness. Still, sometimes we attempt to shoulder that burden again, convincing ourselves that we can never be free from its weight. But Christ longs for us to embrace the freedom he offers, accepting his gift of grace.

When Adam and Eve sinned, they felt immediate shame because they were uncovered (Genesis 3:6-7). But we who place our trust in Christ are covered by the blood of the Lamb. As you consider your own shortcomings as a mom, it can be helpful to understand the difference between guilt and shame. Godly guilt says, "I have done wrong." When we sin in motherhood, the Spirit invites us to turn back to him. His kindness leads us to repentance, and he will never turn us away. Unfortunately, we can quickly slip from guilt into shame, which says, "I *am* wrong." But this can never be true, because Jesus has dealt with our shame once and for all and given us a new name and identity. We are now daughters of the King, who are fully righteous on his account, made right in God's eyes (2 Corinthians 5:21)! This is what it means to be justified (Romans 5:18).

Sister, if you are in Christ, you no longer have to hang your head in shame every time you fail. While our sin carries consequences, even our ugliest parenting mistakes cannot hinder God's plan for us or for our children. Instead, he mercifully lifts your eyes to him and says, "I am taking your imperfect record, and I'm giving you the spotless record of my Son Jesus. I am clothing you in his perfect robes of righteousness. You are forgiven. You are clean."

If you have failed today as a mom, pray to God who is ready to forgive you. Ask your children for forgiveness, allowing them to see what it looks like to acknowledge failure and repent. Then, walk forward in freedom and remember, "There is now no condemnation for those in Christ," who have been freed from the guilt of the law (Romans 8:1-2). He will not cast you out, but like the Father of the prodigal son, he will run to you when you turn back to him— embracing, kissing, robing you to cover your shame and welcoming you back into the family (Luke 15:11-32).

You can never exhaust the grace and kindness of God. Let these words of hope wash over you: "I am sure that neither death nor life, nor angels nor rulers, nor things present nor things to come, nor powers, nor height nor depth, nor anything else in all creation, will be able to separate us from the love of God in Christ Jesus our Lord" (Romans 8:38-39).

When You're Tempted
Toward Laziness

Whatever you do, work at it with all your heart, as working for the Lord, not for human masters, since you know that you will receive an inheritance from the Lord as a reward. It is the Lord Christ you are serving.

COLOSSIANS 3:23-24 NIV

Excel in the unseen." These convicting words startled me awake one morning. I knew they were from the Lord, because excelling in the unseen isn't my natural bent. Frankly, I excel in the *seen,* readily offering advice and encouragement from behind a computer screen and showcasing the good fruit of my parenting. I'm quick to invite you to my home when it's sparkling clean and smells of fresh-baked bread. But I am not as eager to devote myself to the humble tasks that no one on this side of heaven sees or appreciates—the daily chores, the small acts of kindness, the quiet sacrifices.

So I knelt in prayer and uttered these words: "Father, help me excel in the unseen work of motherhood today: to serve my family with humility, to disciple my kids with joy, and to perform the menial tasks of motherhood without grumbling." I did not anticipate the countless opportunities God would give me to practice excelling in the unseen that day. (Isn't that often the case?)

If you're like me, you're always looking for the next hack that will make parenting easier. But, as they say, Rome wasn't built in a day, and neither are the hearts, minds, and characters of our children. Over a decade of motherhood has taught me that diligence is a powerful virtue in parenting. Diligently following through in discipline—letting your yes be yes and your no be no (Matthew 5:37)—reaps obedient, enjoyable children who respect boundaries and authority. Diligence in eating well and exercising regularly bears the fruit of clear minds and healthy bodies. So when someone asks, "How did you teach your children to read? How did they become helpful around the house? How did you find your daily rhythm as a mom?" The answer is the same: taking small, intentional, consistent steps toward a goal that will one day bear fruit. There's no shortcut to replace daily diligence, but the long-term benefits are immeasurably rewarding.

But here's the problem: despite our best efforts, none of us can be perfectly diligent. We grow tired, discouraged, and lose sight of the goal. Praise God for his perfect, never-giving-up, steadfast love that fills in the gaps. He faithfully produces fruit even through our imperfect efforts. He is our Keeper, even when we feel lazy and ready to give up.

Elisabeth Elliot popularized the poem "Do the Next Thing."[1] It reminds those who are overwhelmed that God is simply asking them to trust him and do the next thing that lies before them. Perhaps those four words spoken aloud—"Do the next thing!"—can serve as a reminder to anchor your hope in Christ and do the next thing he has given you to do.

And so, friend, let us be "steadfast, immovable, always abounding in the work of the Lord, knowing that in the Lord your labor is not in vain" (1 Corinthians 15:58). Let's choose one area today in which to exercise diligence, even when we're not in the mood. And let's watch the Lord slowly, assuredly bear fruit.

Sisters, we aren't working toward earthly accolades. We won't receive a bonus for how patiently we handled our child's tantrum or endured another sleepless night with a colicky baby. But we serve Christ the King. And our faithfulness to him—despite being unseen by the world—is seen by the one who matters.

DO THE NEXT THING

by Mrs. George A. Paull

From an old English parsonage down by the sea
There came in the twilight a message to me;
Its quaint Saxon legend, deeply engraven,
Hath, it seems to me, teaching from Heaven.
And on through the doors the quiet words ring
Like a low inspiration: "Do the next thing."
Many a questioning, many a fear,
Many a doubt, hath its quieting here.
Moment by moment, let down from Heaven,
Time, opportunity, and guidance are given.
Fear not tomorrows, child of the King,
Trust them with Jesus, do the next thing.
Do it immediately, do it with prayer;
Do it reliantly, casting all care;
Do it with reverence, tracing His hand

Who placed it before thee with earnest command.
Stayed on Omnipotence, safe 'neath His wing,
Leave all results, do the next thing.
Looking for Jesus, ever serener,
Working or suffering, be thy demeanor;
In His dear presence, the rest of His calm,
The light of His countenance be thy psalm,
Strong in His faithfulness, praise and sing.
Then, as He beckons thee, do the next thing.[2]

BOOK RECOMMENDATION

Everyday Faithfulness: The Beauty of Ordinary Perseverance in a Demanding World by Glenna Marshall

When You Need to
Remember Your Purpose

THE LORD IS YOUR KEEPER

*If Jesus is precious to you, you will not be able to keep your
good news to yourself; you will be whispering it into your
child's ear; you will be telling it to your husband; you will be
earnestly imparting it to your friend; without the charms of
eloquence, you will be more than eloquent; your heart will
speak, and your eyes will flash as you talk of his sweet love.*

CHARLES H. SPURGEON[1]

I used to believe that fulfilling the Great Commission—Jesus's
command to his followers to make disciples of all nations (Matthew 28:18-20; Acts 1:8)—required a packed suitcase, tearful
goodbyes, and strenuous travel to far-off lands. While sometimes it does, the reality is that when the Spirit regenerates your heart,
you cannot help but spread this news. Sharing the gospel is the natural outflow of a heart in love with Jesus. When Jesus told his disciples to make disciples, he instructed them to first spread the word
about him in Jerusalem, their hometown. As a Christian mother,
your immediate family *is* your Jerusalem. No matter the continent
on which you live and serve, your children are your first mission field.

When we understand our calling as Christian mothers to make disciples, we can also appreciate the purpose of our homes. Author Gloria Furman refers to the Christian home as a "little gospel outpost."[2] Beyond providing a place of comfort or expression, your home exists for the people who walk through your doors to hear the good news. It is a command center from which prayers go forth that have the potential to change the world. It is a training ground where we teach the next generation to know and follow Christ.

Sharing the gospel with your kids can feel like a weighty responsibility, but 2 Peter 1:3 assures us that God provides you with everything you need to parent well: "His divine power has given us everything we need for a godly life through our knowledge of him who called us by his own glory and goodness" (NIV). Seeking advice from wise, godly women or reading parenting books rooted in biblical principles can be helpful, but when it comes to making final decisions on parenting, discipline, and your child's future, you and your spouse are the ultimate God-appointed leaders. So walk closely with Jesus, bathe your decisions in prayer, then move forward with confidence, trusting that he will lead you.

Maybe you fight inner voices that make you feel like you could be doing more valuable things with your time. I will admit that the thought has crossed my mind: *How did I go from earning a degree and being a productive member of society to wiping noses, saying "no, no, sweetheart" a dozen times a day, and reading* The Little Blue Truck *until I have it memorized?* But when I look into the eyes of my precious children, I realize that what I'm doing right now is perhaps of greater worth than anything I've ever done. I get to partner with the Holy Spirit to guide and nurture my children's hearts and prepare them for their lives beyond our home. I get to fulfill the Great Commission.

When you spend your days singing to your babies and praying over their futures, you are fulfilling the Great Commission. When you teach your toddlers simple truths like "God made you" and "God loves you," you are fulfilling the Great Commission. When you counsel your teenagers and adult children with biblically rooted wisdom and pray that their decisions will honor Christ, you are fulfilling the Great Commission. We know this because his Word will not return void (Isaiah 55:11). In all these ways, you are planting seeds that will take root and flourish into fruit that lasts for eternity. This is kingdom work.

God has the power to save our children without our help. But he invites us to be an integral part of their faith journey. God chose you for this role, has equipped you for it, and promises to guide you every step of the way as you lean on him.

TEACHING GOD'S WORD TO YOUR CHILDREN

Deuteronomy 6:4-7 tells us clearly: "Hear, O Israel: The LORD our God, the LORD is one. Love the LORD your God with all your heart and with all your soul and with all your strength. These commandments that I give you today are to be on your hearts. Impress them on your children. Talk about them when you sit at home and when you walk along the road, when you lie down and when you get up" (NIV).

What does this look like practically? In our family, it has looked a number of different ways depending on the ages of our kids. We begin our days by reading a Bible story together. For little ones, the *Kingdom of God Bible Storybook* by Lithos Kids or *The Gospel Story Bible* by Marty Machowski are two favorite resources. For older children, you might slowly read a book of the Bible in your favorite translation. Then, depending on their age and readiness, walk through these simple questions together:

1. What does this story tell us about God? What does it say about who he is and what he has done?

2. What does this passage teach us about human beings (or ourselves)? What are we meant to be, and what has gone wrong?

3. How does this passage point us to Jesus? How do we see the need for and the coming of a Savior?

4. How should we respond?

After discussing the Bible passage together, we spend a short time praying, and close by singing a hymn or a worship song. To make this as convenient as possible, we keep a Bible and a hymnal near our breakfast table. Once you've established this daily rhythm, try adding Scripture memory by practicing a verse or two each week. Remember, it doesn't have to be long or complicated to be impactful. The Word of God is living and active (Hebrews 4:12). Nothing is more powerful.

BOOK RECOMMENDATIONS

The Lifegiving Parent: Giving Your Child a Life Worth Living for Christ by Clay and Sally Clarkson

Missional Motherhood: The Everyday Ministry of Motherhood in the Grand Plan of God by Gloria Furman

PART SIX

The Lord Is Your Comfort

The sun shall not strike you by day, nor the moon by night.

PSALM 121:6

I n the sixth verse of Psalm 121, the psalmist draws our attention to the sun and the moon. When this psalm was written, people commonly believed that these celestial bodies were not just inanimate sources of light, but powerful deities that could affect their daily lives. But the psalmist reminds us in this verse that only God has ultimate authority. Nothing that happens, whether in the middle of the day or late at night, is beyond God's control. He is always present, always aware, and always looking after us.

As believers, we have the assurance that, ultimately, nothing can harm us because nothing can separate us from the love of God in Christ Jesus (Romans 8:38-39). The trials we face as moms, whether feelings of depression and anxiety or days that make us question our calling, will not strike us. In other words, they cannot cause real, lasting harm. God is with us; nothing the world throws at us is outside his loving dominion.

When we think of comfort, many of us think of ease. But in stark contrast to this view, Jesus, in John 17, was preparing to give his life

for the sins of the world. Instead of asking for comfort or ease, he selflessly prayed to the Father to keep his followers in his name, protect them from evil, and sanctify them in the truth. Instead of receiving comfort, Jesus was tortured in our place. By giving his life for our sins, he was securing eternal comfort for those who deserved death. The cross shows us just how deep his love is for us!

The only true and lasting comfort we will ever have in life comes from knowing this God, and one of the surest ways to know him is through his Word. From Genesis to Revelation, we see God's glorious plan of redemption unfold. We know the end of the story—he is making all things new!—and this hope for eternal security and rest brings great comfort.

As you read the following devotions, I pray that you will learn to lift your eyes to the one who already has his eyes on you. He is never surprised by your trials or unmoved by your pain. He draws near us with gentleness, compassion, and understanding. He is our great Comforter.

When Life Isn't Going as You Planned

Many are the plans in the mind of a man,
but it is the purpose of the LORD that will stand.

PROVERBS 19:21

Life often throws us curveballs. You may find yourself unexpectedly caring for a family member with special needs, which can leave you feeling overwhelmed. Or your husband suddenly works long shifts and is rarely home to help, a change that can feel isolating. Perhaps you've always dreamed of having a big family, but you don't understand why God hasn't allowed it. Or you're a single mom, and this was never how you anticipated raising your kids. You could even be living the life you always envisioned but discovering it doesn't feel as fulfilling as you hoped.

As a little girl, I dreamed of becoming a missionary in a foreign country. I planned to enter the medical field, so I took college Spanish courses and earned a nursing degree to provide tangible help to those in need. But this dream was never realized. Instead of spending my days in remote villages and serving a cross-cultural community, I spend my days at home in the suburbs, investing in the four young disciples under my care. But when I lift my eyes and ask the Lord for his perspective, he reveals that *this is* his mission for me. He has packed my life with more meaning and purpose than I ever could have produced by myself.

A few years ago, while searching for resources to help me disciple my children, I couldn't find exactly what I was looking for and decided to write my own. Soon, others expressed interest in purchasing the material I had written, and before I knew it, Brighter Day Press was born. Through this ministry, my husband and I create gospel-centered resources that equip and inspire parents to teach their children with confidence, creativity, and truth. Taking a step back, I have realized that many orders we receive are from countries all over the world. Our materials have been translated into multiple languages, reaching places I could never travel to on my own. In his providence, God has allowed me to do cross-cultural ministry in a way I never foresaw. His plan is always better than mine. As Tim Keller once wisely wrote, "God will either give us what we ask or give us what we would have asked if we knew everything he knows."[1]

Some circumstances in life feel perplexing: illnesses, injuries, and emotional scars caused by damaged relationships. But in the midst of pain and confusion, we must say in faith, "Not my will, but yours be done," reminding ourselves that God's ways are always best, even when life isn't going the way we planned. How has he used your trials to comfort others? How has he transformed the death of your dreams into the birth of new ones?

Psalm 136 reminds us that regardless of whether our lives are going according to our plans, God's steadfast love endures forever. The psalmist repeats this refrain 26 times: "for his steadfast love endures forever." As I write this in my thirties, I can already look back and clearly see God's unwavering love woven through every chapter of my story.

I was born into a family who knew Jesus and told me about his love for me, *for his steadfast love endures forever.*

At 16 years old, I was involved in a serious car accident but walked away with only minor injuries, *for his steadfast love endures forever.*

My husband and I endured three painful miscarriages, but in the midst of each one, we experienced God's tender, comforting presence, *for his steadfast love endures forever.*

Our family has made multiple cross-country moves, and amid seasons of loneliness, God sent his people to minister to us in tangible ways, *for his steadfast love endures forever.*

How can you see God's steadfast love woven through your story, even if it isn't going according to your plan? Praise God that you are never left alone to chart the course of your life! His plans for you are good, *for his steadfast, unshakable, unwavering, comforting love endures forever.*

George Matheson, a British pastor, faced the reality of a life of unexpected disappointment. At the age of 20, he was engaged to be married, but had begun to lose his sight. There was nothing the doctors could do to stop his progression toward total blindness. When he broke the news to his fiancée, she decided she could not endure life with a blind husband and broke off their engagement. Twenty years later, Matheson was 40 years old, completely blind, and single.[2] He felt the sting of a life that had not gone as he planned. But in this moment, he clung to God's steadfast love that had carried him and wrote these lyrics that still minister to us today:

> O Love that will not let me go,
> I rest my weary soul in thee.
> I give thee back the life I owe,
> That in thine ocean depths its flow
> May richer, fuller be.[3]

When You're Tempted
to Compare

THE LORD IS YOUR COMFORT

*Turn my eyes from looking at worthless
things; and give me life in your ways.*

PSALM 119:37

One of the nightly traditions I've savored most has been singing to my babies in a rocking chair before bedtime. I sing hymns like "Great Is Thy Faithfulness" and "There Is a Fountain" because I want the truth of the gospel to fill their minds from their earliest memory. But when I've sung all the hymns I can think of and my baby is still wide awake, I dig in the archives of my brain to unearth songs I sang in Sunday school. I sing simple but profound truths from the lyrics of "Jesus Loves the Little Children," "He's Got the Whole World in His Hands," and "Jesus Loves Me."

The other night, I was singing to my youngest son, Beckham,

> O be careful, little eyes, what you see
> O be careful, little eyes, what you see
> For the Father up above is looking down in love
> So be careful, little eyes, what you see.[1]

That night, the lyrics struck me. They reminded me of Philippians 4:8, which admonishes, "whatever is true, whatever is honorable, whatever is just, whatever is pure, whatever is lovely, whatever is commendable, if there is any excellence, if there is anything worthy of praise, think about these things." I realized I needed to hear those lyrics more than my son did.

Nineteenth-century English poet William Blake wrote, "We become what we behold."[2] This raises the question: what are we beholding? To where or to whom are we lifting our eyes? In an age where information is instantly accessible through the smartphones in our hands, are we being mindful about what our eyes see, what our ears hear, and what our minds consume and absorb? This applies not only to the blatant evil we can quickly uncover, but also to the seemingly "good" aspects of the internet too. Beholding another person's life highlights through social media—especially if our own journey has been difficult—can be a one-way ticket to comparison. Gazing at images of well-behaved children, flawless skin, and sunny vacations can stir up feelings of inadequacy and resentment. You've probably heard the phrase, "Comparison is the thief of joy." Whether it's our postpartum bodies or even our children's achievements, women seem particularly prone to the sin of jealousy. As soon as we crave what someone else has, joy slips through our fingers. Peace is far away. Contentment walks out the door.

Comparison in itself is not a sin. Sometimes we look at what others have been given, and the Spirit helps us rejoice at how he is clearly working in their lives. But when comparison leads to jealousy, resentment, or blaming God for what we do not have, we fall into the sin of covetousness (Colossians 3:5).

When we feel tempted to compare, we should be careful about what we choose to see and intentionally take inventory of the many gifts God has already given. The baby in your arms, a steaming cup of tea, clean cotton sheets, laughter—every moment that we have breath in our lungs is a chance to soak in the simple joys God has given us. When we set our gaze on what is right in front of us and literally count our blessings, we acknowledge his benevolence and lavish grace.

BOOK RECOMMENDATION

The Envy of Eve: Finding Contentment in a Covetous World by Melissa
   B. Kruger

When You're Suffering and Need to Know God Is Near

THE LORD IS YOUR COMFORT

Believe in the darkness what you have seen in the light.

LILIAS TROTTER, Missionary to Algeria[1]

The story of Darlene Deibler Rose is harrowing. In her early twenties, Darlene was newly married and sent to the mission field deep in the jungles of New Guinea. But shortly after her ministry began, World War II erupted, and Japanese soldiers invaded the area where she was living. As a result, Darlene and her fellow missionaries were imprisoned in an internment camp. For four heart-wrenching years, Darlene suffered near-starvation, forced labor, illness, interrogation, and the constant threat of death. In her memoir, *Evidence Not Seen,* she admitted she was pushed to the point that she felt she could no longer endure such immense suffering. She wrote,

> I thought God had left me, that He had forsaken me. I was to discover, however, that when I took my eyes off the circumstances that were overwhelming me, over which I had no control, and looked up, my Lord was there,

standing on the parapet of heaven looking down. Deep in my heart He whispered, "I'm here. Even when you don't see Me, I'm here. Never for a moment are you out of My sight."[2]

As Darlene attested, when we lift our eyes off our overwhelming circumstances and onto our Savior, he reminds us of his comforting presence and watchful care. In addition, Jesus doesn't just sit idly while we hurt, indifferent to our pain. He grieves with us. When his friend Lazarus died, Jesus mourned with Mary and Martha, despite having the power to heal Lazarus instantly. Those two words—"Jesus wept" (John 11:35)—demonstrate that he willingly entered our human experience of suffering. Even now, though he may not immediately fix things, he chooses to draw near and bring comfort to us.

Our God is so near to us that the language of the Bible says that through faith we are actually *united* to Christ. We are *in* him and he is *in* us. Listen to these beautiful words and note how many times Paul emphasizes our unity with Christ:

> Blessed be the God and Father of our Lord Jesus Christ, who has blessed us *in Christ* with every spiritual blessing in the heavenly places, even as he chose us *in him* before the foundation of the world, that we should be holy and blameless before him. In love he predestined us for adoption *to himself* as sons through Jesus Christ, according to the purpose of his will, to the praise of his glorious grace, with which he has blessed us *in the Beloved. In him* we have redemption through his blood, the forgiveness of our trespasses, according to the riches of his grace...*In him* we have obtained an inheritance, having been predestined according to the purpose of him who works all things according to the counsel of his will, so that we who were

the first to hope in Christ might be to the praise of his glory. *In him* you also, when you heard the word of truth, the gospel of your salvation, and believed in him, were *sealed with the promised Holy Spirit*, who is the guarantee of our inheritance until we acquire possession of it, to the praise of his glory (Ephesians 1:3-7, 11-14, emphases mine).

Sister, remember that God has united himself to you; he has bound himself to you in Christ. He can never be closer to you than he already is. Whether you are receiving bad news in a doctor's office, enduring a season of loss, or feeling the weight of motherhood, lift your eyes to your Comforter. He is nearer to you than your shadow and comforts you in every affliction.

PSALMS OF COMFORT

When you're suffering and need to know that God is near, the psalms can be a balm to your hurting heart. Choose one of the following psalms, read it slowly, and pray that God would give you the faith to believe these words: Psalm 13, Psalm 31, Psalm 37, Psalm 91, Psalm 94, Psalm 103, or Psalm 142. Rehearse his astounding benefits to you and remind your soul that he graciously draws near to you in your suffering.

BOOK RECOMMENDATIONS

God's Grace In Your Suffering by David Powlison

Suffering Is Never for Nothing by Elisabeth Elliot

When You Struggle to Love Your Children Well

Let love be genuine. Abhor what is evil; hold fast
to what is good. Love one another with brotherly
affection. Outdo one another in showing honor.

ROMANS 12:9-10

A few years ago, I woke up with a mile-long to-do list and some hiccups in our small business. Feeling stretched thin, I called my mom, as I often do. After listening to me, she encouraged me to put the business problems aside for now and focus on the most urgent need in front of me: my four young children. She said, "Let this be your act of worship." While there were other pressing matters demanding my attention, I knew that ignoring my kids would harm them and our relationship in the long run. My mom reminded me that investing fully in the tiny disciples at my feet was an act of faith and trust. Romans 12 urges us to present ourselves as living sacrifices to God, for this is our spiritual worship. This reframing of my perspective brought relief and clarity, and I realized that being fully present with my kids was a way of trusting and worshipping God. The other tasks could wait until naptime.

Cleaning up LEGOs, mopping spilled juice, or correcting a child for the tenth time may not feel like acts of worship. But oh, how Jesus delights to meet us in humble places! In his unparalleled humility, Jesus showed us how to live by putting others before ourselves. And as humans prone to put ourselves first, it's perhaps the hardest lesson to learn.

Though we love our children dearly, it's hard to put their needs before our own. It can even be a struggle to look at them and to not see their sin and weakness first. We tend to apply labels to our children based on their most prevalent or irritating sins and say things like: "Oh, that's Henry...he's always whiny." "She's high-strung." "He's difficult." "She is such a handful." But not only do these labels leave no room for change, they are simply not how Jesus addressed people. As followers of Christ, we can learn from his example. He chose to spend his time with those the religious crowds would never associate with: prostitutes, tax collectors, and people many considered to be the dregs of society. He called them not by what they had done, but by name.

"Mary," not "prostitute."

"Matthew," not "tax collector."

Jesus looked them in the eye. He shared meals with them and washed their dirty feet. And in doing so, he blessed them with dignity and value.

As we follow Christ's example and receive his strength, we can see our children as image bearers of God, and doing so can transform our parenting—and our children. Instead of first looking at my child's neediness, sometimes evidenced by whininess or bickering, I see him as a precious soul who is deeply loved by God. I see her struggling with a sin but not defined by it. I see them with eyes of hope.

Proverbs 22:6 is an often-quoted verse about parenting, and

rightly so: "Train up a child in the way he should go; even when he is old, he will not depart from it." This verse is often interpreted: "Teach your kids about God, pray with them, and never miss a Sunday at church, and they'll never wander from God or doubt his presence." But this interpretation does not accurately reflect the meaning of the verse.

In the original Hebrew, this proverb can be more accurately translated "Train him up his way" or according to his unique inner bent.[1] In other words, listen to your child. Appreciate the one-of-a-kind uniqueness of your child. Trust that God didn't make a mistake when he created him or her to like certain things or behave in certain ways, and prayerfully parent them accordingly. In this way, we are calling our child by his "name" and acknowledging his deeper, God-given identity. We choose to see our child where he is in that moment, with limitless hope for the future.

There will be plenty of days when we struggle to love our children well or put their needs ahead of ours. On those days, let's lift our eyes to Christ, who always sees us with eyes of hope, and helps us see our children with his vision too.

When You Are Grieving

THE LORD IS YOUR COMFORT

Just as we share abundantly in the sufferings of Christ,
so also our comfort abounds through Christ.

2 CORINTHIANS 1:5 NIV

Time of death, 10:35 p.m.* In my work as a nurse, I have heard doctors announce a patient's time of death dozens of times. Whether the person's passing was expected or not, the moment was always somber as medical personnel stepped away from the lifeless body in a hush of silence.

But this was different. This time, I wasn't standing beside a hospital bed; I was crouched on my bathroom floor. Heavy bleeding had begun during my pregnancy, and I knew exactly what it meant. In a cloud of hormones and grief, I thought that if my baby didn't have a name and would never celebrate a birthday, at least I should know the time that marked the end of his or her earthly life.

On this sweltering June night, I was suffering my third miscarriage. This pregnancy had come as a complete surprise, and it had taken me and my husband a few weeks to wrap our minds around the gift of a fourth child. But we had. And it seemed that as soon as we let ourselves get excited, the strange sense that we wouldn't meet this baby on this side of heaven crept over me. I called my doctor and reported no other symptoms besides a nagging feeling that something was off. He asked me to come to his office to have my blood drawn and, a few hours later, delivered grim news: My hormone levels were far from what they should be at nine weeks of pregnancy. I would likely miscarry within a few days. Mercifully, that painful, heartbreaking process began at 10:35 p.m. that night.

Even if you've already experienced a miscarriage, the emotional pain of a second, third, or fourth loss doesn't get easier. After each loss, I've yearned more deeply for Christ to return and obliterate death forever. But also, the promise of heaven becomes more precious and palpable when I envision our perfectly whole loved ones waiting for us there.

As we study the Bible, we learn of countless men and women who had reasons to grieve. One of them was the writer of the book of Lamentations. As the wicked King Nebuchadnezzar of Babylon laid siege to Jerusalem in 586 BC, the prophet Jeremiah penned this book. He recounted that no one inside the city walls could escape, and no food or supplies from the outside could make it in. The atrocities he described are shocking, heavy, and seem hopeless. And yet, he found hope. But where? How? He wrote, "Because of the LORD's great love, we are not consumed" (Lamentations 3:22 NIV). The Hebrew word for this type of love is *hesed*. This is a deeply committed, covenant love—not a "give and take" kind of love, but a "give and give and give" kind of love. It is not based on the worthiness of the one who is loved but on the lover, who is the Lord. God's love is an unbreakable, one-way kind of love (Romans 5:7-8), which finds its source in his generous, unchanging character.

If you've endured loss as I have, you may question God's generosity. It might feel like he has only taken away. I can attest that amid deep pain, God always gives us himself. The prophet Isaiah wrote, "Surely, he has borne our griefs and carried our sorrows" (Isaiah 53:4). Jesus himself has shouldered our hurt and offers his comforting presence in ways we may never know outside of suffering.

Through these experiences of loss, I have known the Lord's tender comfort in unexpected ways: through friends who wrote Scriptures on notecards and placed them all over the house so I would dwell on truth in my weakest moments; through loved ones who quietly sat with me in my sadness and interceded for me as I was rolled into surgery after my body failed to complete the miscarriage; and through my doctor who walked through each phase of loss with genuine compassion.

God showed himself to me as Immanuel—"God with us"—so that even amid great pain, I was never alone. He is your Immanuel too. *God with you* on the exam table as you gaze upon a still, silent ultrasound screen. *God with you* as you trust him with your family's future. *God with you,* choosing to enter your pain, to carry your grief, and to flood your broken heart with incomprehensible hope. Let's lift our eyes to the one who comforts us as we grieve.

WALKING THROUGH GRIEF

I want to share some words of encouragement I've gleaned from various losses. I pray these truths bring hope to you or someone you know who is grieving.

1. We won't fully understand God's sovereign ways this
   side of heaven, but we can trust his character. He is a
   wise, loving Father, even in the midst of great pain. Even

when God's plans don't make sense to us, they are for our ultimate good and for his glory.

2. Jesus grieves with you, and he has experienced grief beyond what we ever will. Hebrews 2:17 (NIV) reminds us, "For this reason he had to be made like them, *fully human in every way*, in order that he might become a merciful and faithful high priest in service to God, and that he might make atonement for the sins of the people" (emphasis added). Jesus understands our pain because he endured it himself, and he offers his presence to us as we grieve.

3. For believers, death does not have the final word. Our glorious, eternal future with God is the hope we cling to! Heaven becomes more tangible when we think of our believing loved ones who have passed away and are now experiencing peace, contentment, and joy that surpasses anything this world offers.

BOOK RECOMMENDATIONS

Held: 31 Biblical Reflections on God's Comfort and Care in the Sorrow of Miscarriage by Abbey Wedgeworth

Inheritance of Tears: Trusting the Lord of Life When Death Visits the Womb by Jessalyn Hutt

PART SEVEN

The Lord Is Your Shepherd

The Lord will keep you from all evil; he will keep your life.

PSALM 121:7

s you reflect on the phrase, "The Lord will keep you from all evil," you may question how such a promise could possibly be true. We all bear the scars of this life, and even Jesus acknowledges in John 16:33 that in this world, we *will* have trouble. Maybe even now, you're walking through a season of profound hardship, such as the loss of a loved one, a complex medical diagnosis, or the betrayal of a friend.

The point of Psalm 121:7 is not that the effects of sin and evil won't touch us. Rather, the psalmist reminds us that the Lord himself will safeguard our souls. You can be confident that Jesus, your Shepherd, is not surprised by what you are going through. He is not standing on the sidelines, wondering what to do next. The afflictions he permits are intended to strengthen your faith, not to shatter it. The suffering and evil that may touch your life are still under his sovereign control. Because of this, you can face these challenging days knowing that your Shepherd is there and will keep you.

Psalm 23 vividly portrays our Lord as our Shepherd. In ancient times, a shepherd's staff was curved like a hook to keep the sheep on

It is one thing to have a shepherd,
but it is an utterly staggering thing
to have as a shepherd the one who is strength itself,
who never tires, never slumbers,
and who never needs protection himself.

DAVID GIBSON[1]

the right path, protecting them from their wanderings. The shepherd's rod was a weapon to defend the sheep from their enemies. In the same way, God guides and protects us, both ensuring we stay on the right path and defending us from harm.

When our work as mothers seems fruitless, the Lord is our Shepherd. When we feel the sting of loneliness, the Lord is our Shepherd. He is always there, observing, preserving, and guiding us, his beloved sheep. Like the psalmist, we can confidently sing that God will not allow evil to harm our souls. As Charles Spurgeon wrote, "If the soul be kept all is kept."[2]

BOOK RECOMMENDATIONS

The Lord of Psalm 23: Jesus Our Shepherd, Companion, and Host by David Gibson

A Shepherd Looks at Psalm 23: Discovering God's Love For You by W. Phillip Keller

When You Doubt Your Ability to Mother Well

THE LORD IS YOUR SHEPHERD

Praise be to the LORD, to God our Savior,
who daily bears our burdens.

PSALM 68:19 NIV

In 2004, a surprising phenomenon occurred when a sheep was found living alone in a cave in New Zealand. This sheep, named Shrek, managed to escape from his enclosure and the care of his shepherd for six years and was, miraculously, still alive. When Shrek was discovered, he was hardly recognizable. His wool coat had grown large and become matted, with dirt and droppings entangled in it. Though it may sound like a funny situation, it was quite desperate.

Shrek was a Merino sheep that required annual shearing. Without the consistent removal of their wool, these sheep can become sick or even die from overheating due to their inability to regulate their body temperature. When Shrek was finally found and returned to his flock, he could barely walk, eat, or function because his heavy coat had weighed him down beyond what he was meant to bear.[1]

In the Bible, people are often compared to sheep, and God is referred to as our Shepherd. Just like Shrek the sheep, when we stray from the loving care of our Shepherd and neglect to spend regular time with him, we find ourselves burdened with worries and fears we were never meant to carry.

Are you feeling weighed down today? Maybe you're doubting that you're cut out for motherhood. You might be feeling a little like Shrek, whose coat grew out of control because he avoided the care of his shepherd.

More than any other experience, being a mom has revealed how much I need someone to guide, care for, and protect me. Motherhood is demanding in every way, but I believe the Lord has not only given you these tasks, but equipped you for them.

When you doubt your ability to mother well, think of the many ways the Lord was preparing you, even long before you became a mom. Before I had children, I worked as a nurse on a busy hospital unit. Some days, I cared for up to seven patients at a time. It felt like a real-life game of Whac-a-Mole: as soon as I tackled one need, another would immediately pop up, and I would race down the hall toward it. I look back now and smile, because I realize that this was one way that God was preparing me to handle having four children in six years. He was equipping me for a future I had no way of foreseeing.

In the same way, he is your good Shepherd too. He chose you to be his beloved sheep and has uniquely prepared you to be your children's mother. Invite him to help you cast off your doubts and insecurities, embracing the freedom of one who is known and helped by him.

I have recently memorized a portion of Romans 8 because it is so foundational to our faith. On the days when I doubt my ability to mother well, the Lord draws those verses out of my memory bank and slips them into my heart:

> The Spirit helps us in our weakness. For we do not know what to pray as we ought, but the Spirit himself intercedes for us with groanings too deep for words (verse 26).

> And we know that for those who love God all things work together for good, for those who are called according to his purpose (verse 28).

> What then shall we say to these things? If God is for us, who can be against us? He who did not spare his own Son but gave him up for us all, how will he not also with him graciously give us all things? (verses 31-32).

When the wool has grown thick around you, return to the only perfect Shepherd, Jesus Christ. Let him shear off the burden of being a perfect mom. Lean into what God has called you to be—a mom who points her children to Jesus.

When You See No Results from the Work You're Putting In

So we do not lose heart. Though our outer self is wasting away, our inner self is being renewed day by day. For this light momentary affliction is preparing for us an eternal weight of glory beyond all comparison, as we look not to the things that are seen but to the things that are unseen. For the things that are seen are transient, but the things that are unseen are eternal.

2 CORINTHIANS 4:16-18

On our smoothest mornings as a family, you might peer through fingerprinted windowpanes to witness us reading a Bible story together, singing a hymn, or practicing a memory verse. You'd also likely spot a child climbing on the table, a piece of toast on the floor, and some crayon marks on the wall. You'd probably hear a silly question that humorously diverts the conversation from the topic at hand.

But what you can't see—and what we often fail to remember—is the spiritual battle that is being waged as we seek to disciple our kids. We battle not against flesh and blood. We aren't fighting against our children's interruptions or even our own flawed attitudes. As you share God's Word with your kids, don't be surprised when it feels like you're fighting a strong headwind: no one is listening, someone spills their drink, or your kids would rather play outside. It's easy to feel like your efforts are futile and to grow weary, distracted, or disheartened. The enemy loves to sow seeds of doubt that what you're doing matters at all. He aims to steal, kill, and destroy the truth you seek to impart (John 10:10), and he works 24-7 to keep our children from hearing the only message that is "the power of God for salvation to everyone who believes" (Romans 1:16).

Our son, Bear, loves the book *Little Pilgrim's Big Journey* by Tyler van Halteren and has asked me to read it to him countless times. One day, as we reached the pivotal scene when Christian's burden falls off his back at the foot of the cross, Bear gasped in a moment of sudden realization, "Can Jesus take my sin burden too?" Dozens of times, reading this story to Bear had seemed pointless. He would often be distracted, his siblings would interrupt us, or someone would need a snack. But unbeknownst to me, God was gradually, steadily opening his eyes to the message of the gospel. Our faithful Shepherd is always present, working through our small acts of faith, even when we can't perceive it.

Even though Scripture does not reveal to us the day-to-day lives of mothers in the Bible, it shows us how God worked in and through them to impact their children's lives. Eunice and Lois—mother and grandmother of Timothy—selflessly dedicated themselves to teaching the Scriptures to Timothy from childhood, allowing Paul to write, "Continue in what you have learned and have firmly believed" (2 Timothy 3:14). This does not mean Timothy inherited his faith, but that these godly women paved the way by spiritually leading Timothy in his younger years. They may not have seen the fruit of this work while they were still alive; however, it is because of Timothy that the gospel spread to new parts of the world. What a rich legacy!

Maybe you feel like you're falling short or not doing enough. Remember this: we were never meant to meet every one of our children's needs. God simply calls us to obey him. In this season, that might look like folding another load of laundry without groaning, teaching a math lesson with patience, or reading a Bible story to the child on your lap. God can achieve big, lasting things with small, unseen offerings because there is no limit to what he can do. Trust that your Shepherd is with you, guiding your every step, and leave the eternal results to him.

When You Need Wisdom for How to Parent

If any of you lacks wisdom, let him ask God, who gives generously to all without reproach, and it will be given him.

JAMES 1:5

A few years ago, I found myself in the middle of a chaotic day with my three children. While the details have faded, I distinctly remember corralling the older two kids into the bathtub, hoping for a moment of peace.

But the peace didn't last long. As I stirred spaghetti sauce on the stove, I suddenly heard the plink, plink, plink of water dripping down our wooden stairs. The kids had mischievously overflowed the bathtub until soapy water sloshed out of the bathroom and down the stairs, streaming into the kitchen where I was standing.

I was angry, exasperated, and at the end of my rope, but I knew if I acted on those emotions, I would regret it. In the past, I had failed tests like this one miserably. But this time, I paused to pray for wisdom before letting myself react. James 1:5 tells us that we should ask God for wisdom if we lack it, and he will generously provide it. I desperately needed my good Shepherd to guide me, and by his grace, the Holy Spirit immediately spoke to me in my weakness. Before my heart could fill with rage, he gently whispered that my children needed something radically merciful to grab their attention. He reminded me that they are sinners, just like me. And he prompted me with an idea.

I grabbed a stack of towels, helped the kids out of the bath, asked them to mop up their mess, then instructed them to go sit on their beds. As they did, I wrote love notes to them. Yes, love notes—not because my heart overflowed with affection, but because God had sparked this idea, and I couldn't ignore it.

I wrote, "Lanie, you make our life so fun! I love to hear you sing, and I'm proud of the amazing big sister you are. I'm grateful every day that you're my daughter." And, "Liam, thank you for making me a mom. It's my favorite job in the world! You are brilliant and kind, and I am delighted when I see the young man you're becoming."

Choosing to show grace in that moment didn't exempt my kids from their earthly consequences. They still had to clean up their mess and apologize for disobeying. But I wanted them to catch a glimpse of their Father's tender heart. I longed for them to understand that his grace is more powerful than their rebellion. I hoped they would taste the mercy that I had first encountered when I came to faith in Christ—that even when I deserved God's wrath, I was met with his grace and forgiveness. This is the power that can soften even the hardest heart. It's his kindness that leads us to repentance (Romans 2:4).

When I entered Liam and Lanie's bedroom, their crestfallen faces revealed that they knew they had disappointed me and expected my anger. Instead, I surprised them by smiling and reading the love notes I had written for each of them. As I did, tears streamed down my face as I felt God's love for *me* in a fresh way. This moment marked a profound shift in my parenting. When the Spirit prompted me to behold my own sin and to recognize the mercy I had been shown, I was able to extend mercy to my son and daughter. That day became a banner moment for my kids too. As much as they could understand at their ages, they grasped that they were truly, wholly forgiven and loved. Their chins lifted, their shoulders relaxed, and they reached toward me instead of cowering in shame.

The Lord is our Shepherd, guiding us as moms as we guide our children. When you lack wisdom, as we often do in parenting, stop what you're doing and pray. Ask your Father for guidance. You can say, "Lord, I feel lost and don't know what to do next. I am angry and bewildered, and I know that I cannot please you in my own strength. Please help me. I trust you to shepherd me as I shepherd my children. Amen."

When Your Affections
for God Feel Weak

THE LORD IS YOUR SHEPHERD

*A renewal of the soul takes place in seeing afresh who I am in
the world—not master and commander but a frail and prone-
to-wander sheep with a good shepherd—and that my experience
of soul rest will always be dependent on my proximity to him.*

DAVID GIBSON[1]

Many believers walk through seasons of spiritual apathy. We know that studying God's Word, praying, and memorizing Scripture is good for us, but our hearts can feel distant from God. Our Bibles gather dust on the shelf, and we feel guilt rather than delight when we think about opening them again.

This was my experience in the early months after my first son was born. I knew I needed to spend time with Jesus—my soul felt dry—but I was sleep-deprived and lacked the focus to pour into any deep study. In demanding seasons of motherhood, you may feel the same way. Our "quiet times" are rarely quiet with the near-constant needs of our children, and it's tempting to give up.

But the truth is, on these taxing days, we need God's Word and his presence more than ever. The roadblocks to spending time with the Lord are many—our children's needs, our limited brain space, our own exhaustion—and these can become excuses for not engaging in Scripture, praying, or going to church most weeks. But these are avenues through which God has chosen to bless you. And when you walk in them, you position yourself to be transformed by his power. You will be blessed because you're standing in the paths of blessing!

When I walk through seasons of spiritual indifference, two words help me draw near to the Lord: *pray* and *abide*.

First, pray. Seek God's help, asking that he stir your affection for him, awakening the joy you once knew. Remember that it doesn't matter how long it's been since you last spent time with him—he is your good Shepherd and is always ready to hear from you. Romans 8:34 tells us that Jesus himself prays and intercedes for you. What a thought! Even when we feel ashamed or weak, our Shepherd is still praying for us.

Second, abide in God's Word. If you're like me, you want to set the stage for a picture-perfect quiet time with hot tea, calming music, and a cozy blanket. But you may have only five minutes before the kids come tumbling downstairs. Perhaps you keep a Bible open on your kitchen counter to meditate on a verse or two when you're stirring oatmeal or waiting for something to bake in the oven.

Depending on the demands of the season you are in, find creative ways to consistently connect with God. Play worship music while making dinner, or write your favorite Scriptures on notecards and place them around the house to remind yourself of truth. These simple practices can allow you to experience God's comforting presence even when you cannot spend as much time in the Word as you would like.

When we lift our eyes to Jesus, our good Shepherd, we gain a new perspective on all of life. We see how things are and the way they should be. In Christ, we behold a love that compels us to love others with the strength he provides.

GROWING SPIRITUALLY

God gives us the spiritual disciplines, including Scripture reading, prayer, and Scripture memory, as a means of his grace. They are provided to us for our benefit, with the goals of enjoying God and growing in godliness.

Bible Reading

If you desire to begin reading the Bible, I recommend using a chronological Bible reading plan like *The Bible Recap* to help you read through the Bible in a year, or however long it takes.[2] Find a friend who will journey alongside you and hold you accountable for seeking God through his Word. I also enjoy listening to the Bible while I go on a walk, scrub dishes, or put on makeup using the Dwell audio Bible app.

Prayer

Prayer is simply pouring out our hearts to God; it does not have to be complicated or long-winded. One simple way to pray is to read or memorize Scripture and offer it back to God. Psalm 121:1-2 says, "I lift up my eyes to the hills. From where does my help come? My help comes from the LORD, who made heaven and earth." We can remember these words and pray them back to the Father, saying, "Lord, these hills feel like mountains. [Name your hills, confessing your fears.] I trust that my help comes from you. You made all things and are sovereign over all. I pray that you will remove the fear in my heart and replace it with your peace."

Scripture Memory

One tool that has helped me to memorize Scripture is to write down the first letter of each word to help commit a verse or passage to memory. Read the passage in full, then use the first-letter technique to recite it a few times each day until you have it memorized.

BOOK RECOMMENDATIONS

Prayer: Experiencing Awe and Intimacy with God by Tim Keller

A Praying Life: Connecting with God in a Distracting World by Paul E. Miller

The Valley of Vision: A Collection of Puritan Prayers and Devotions by Arthur Bennett

Women of the Word: How to Study the Bible with Both Our Hearts and Our Minds by Jen Wilkin

When Church Hurts

*May a merciful God preserve me from a Christian Church
in which everyone is a saint! I want to be and remain in
the church and little flock of the fainthearted, the feeble
and the ailing, who feel and recognize the wretchedness
of their sins, who sigh and cry to God incessantly for
comfort and help, who believe in the forgiveness of sins.*

MARTIN LUTHER[1]

As someone who was brought up in the church and spent a
decade as a pastor's wife, I have faced my share of church
hurt. There were Sundays when, on our drive home, I told
my husband, in all sincerity, "I never want to set foot
in that church again." Though I was aware that never returning to
church was not a healthy or viable option, I've sometimes allowed a
shell to grow cold and hard around my heart, deciding not to let anyone from a particular church community get too close.

And do you know what happened?

I missed out on so much. I allowed an experience with one person to taint my perception of an entire body of believers. As a result, I
missed the chance to know or be known by them. I lost the redemptive opportunity to forgive and to experience what a church is—a

group of imperfect people striving to know and love Jesus and one another.

Sadly, my experience is all too common. Maybe you, like me, have grown roots in a church family but have been deeply hurt. Perhaps you've longed for a church that is always safe and comforting. But the sin of imperfect people slices through that image and cuts shards in your heart. Your experience may go beyond being judged by another mom in the nursing mothers' room or feeling excluded by a clique of women. You may have suffered physical or emotional abuse. Depending on your experience, healing and restoring trust can be slow, painful work, requiring discernment and boundaries.

Though I've been hurt by various churches in the past and have done my share of wounding, I've also been moved by the beauty of the body of Christ. Throughout most of our married life, my husband and I have lived far away from our extended family and have relied on our church to be our brothers and sisters, moms and dads. I have been discipled by older, wiser women who have generously shared their wisdom. In addition, fellow church members have demonstrated their love for us by dropping off meals when we're sick, watching our home when we're out of town, or caring for our kids so we can enjoy a much-needed date. When our family moved from North Carolina to Texas, a community group we hardly knew stocked our pantry with every item we needed. And when my husband, Shawn, suffered a serious accident, four families from our church were by our side within minutes.

When you make it a priority to gather with fellow believers at church, it matters not only to you; it matters to your children. Your kids see the high value you place on fellowship with the body of Christ, working week after hard week through chaos and "where in the world are a pair of matching socks?" to get to church. They have a front-row seat to your obedience to God's command in Hebrews 10:25 not to forsake meeting together. Watching the church service at home in your sweats with a cup of coffee would be more convenient, and sometimes a season or circumstance calls for that. But one way Jesus loves us is through other people. More than ever, we need in-person relationships. We need real hugs, accountability, and encouragement from our brothers and sisters. We need other believers to remind us of truth and hope when we struggle to believe it for ourselves. No church is perfect, but it is God's vehicle for community, sanctification, and growth. Pastor Tim Keller once made the bold statement, "Only if you are part of a community of believers seeking to resemble, serve, and love Jesus will you ever get to know him and grow into his likeness."[2]

When church hurts, lift your eyes to your faithful Shepherd, who understands your deepest wounds. Ask him to meet you in your Sunday morning brokenness, and watch for the ways he may want to minister to you through the imperfect love of his people. Even when others let us down, he will remain faithful.

PART EIGHT

The Lord Is Your Sustainer

The LORD will keep your going out and your coming
in from this time forth and forevermore.

PSALM 121:8

A s we reach the final verse of Psalm 121, we rejoice that the Lord is our Sustainer. This is good news because not only has he supported and guarded us in the past, but he promises to keep us "from this time forth and forevermore." Jesus Christ is the same yesterday, today, and forever (Hebrews 13:8), and if you are united to Christ by faith, his care for you never ends.

Not only that, but "your going out and your coming in" includes every aspect of your life as a mom. God is there to sustain you when you are overstimulated and overwhelmed or when you feel like you've blown it and need a fresh start. You can lift your eyes to God's sustaining presence even when battling grief, fear, or sheer exhaustion.

The people and seasons of your life will inevitably change over time. Your children will grow into adults and leave your home, and you yourself will grow older and face new freedoms and challenges in

your relationships. You may experience suffering along the way, but you can trust that God's unchanging nature and promises go before you, so there is no need to fear the future. In reality, your future is incredibly bright! As missionary Adoniram Judson once said, "He has not led me so tenderly thus far to forsake me at the very gate of heaven."[1] Under this kind of protection, you can walk through motherhood without fear, knowing God will sustain you every step of the way.

Someday we will be able to see God as he already sees us. "For now we see in a mirror dimly, but then face to face. Now I know in part; then I shall know fully, even as I have been fully known" (1 Corinthians 13:12). Until then, we can echo the psalmist in proclaiming, "Surely God is my help; the Lord is the one who sustains me" (Psalm 54:4 NIV).

When You're Having
a Rough Day

THE LORD IS YOUR SUSTAINER

I will give you a new heart, and a new spirit I will
put within you. And I will remove the heart of stone
from your flesh and give you a heart of flesh.

EZEKIEL 36:26

Our family has a silly, unspoken house rule: we don't mix playdough colors. This was established by our oldest son as a preschooler because he preferred playing with clean colors instead of a mashed-up brown blob. When I saw him add a tiny piece of green playdough to the yellow one day, I was surprised and looked on.

His tiny fingers kneaded and smashed the dough, slowly at first, then furiously. I watched disappointment cloud his eyes when he realized the green wasn't going away. He brought the marbled yellow dough to me and said, "Mama, I just want it to be yellow again. What if we add some yellow food coloring?"

"Oh, buddy," I said, "that's a good idea, but even that isn't going to take out the green."

But I could see his determination: he had to try this for himself.

I reluctantly pulled out a bowl, a spoon, and yellow food coloring. With gritted teeth, he mixed the yellow-green wad of playdough with fervor, but still saw flecks of green. Watching him, I was reminded of a spiritual truth.

"Hey buddy, you know how we talk about sin and that only Jesus can forgive us and make us clean?" I asked.

"Yes," he whispered as he continued to knead the dough.

"Let's act like the little bit of green is sin. Maybe you told a lie, or maybe I acted angrily toward you. Instead of running straight to Jesus, confessing, and asking him to make us clean again, we try to cover it up. We mash the dough and try to hide it by mixing it in. And does that work?"

Liam shook his head as I continued the analogy, comparing the yellow food coloring to the good works we sometimes try to add to cover up our sin.

"But here's the thing," I explained. "Jesus loves us so much that he doesn't want us to stay in our sin. When we ask for his forgiveness, he gives us a clean heart: a perfectly yellow piece of playdough. We will mess up over and over, and he will clean our mess again and again."

I assured Liam that in the same way I didn't expect him to keep his playdough completely clean, God knows we cannot keep our hearts completely clean either. His Word tells us that we all sin and fall short of God's glory (Romans 3:23). I anticipate that Liam will make mistakes. But I hope he will run to Jesus in repentance and accept the newness of heart God offers.

A few days after this conversation, I had a low moment in the drive-thru line. It had been a tough day with a fussy baby, and my older kids were begging for ice cream *cones*—not cups—that they hoped I could balance while driving 20 minutes home. On top of that, our order was wrong. So I sat there, holding up the drive-thru line with three sobbing children in the backseat. In an effort to appease them, I tossed a kid's meal in their direction where it landed short, tumbled out of my children's reach, and scattered fries all over the floorboard. This was clearly a small problem in the order of things, like a speck of green in the yellow playdough. But I grumbled, *If only I could have more sleep, I'd be able to cope. If only we had extended family who lived closer, I'd get a break. I need more help, more money, more rest.*

Then, from the driver's seat of my minivan, a sense of calmness and rest flooded my heart as I heard the voice of Truth: *What you need is a new heart.* As in the moment with Liam, God was graciously and faithfully parenting me in the midst of my frustration, right there in the drive-thru line. *Yes, Lord. A new heart.*

> He who was seated on the throne said,
> "Behold, I am making all things new."
> Revelation 21:5

Revelation's promise of "all things new" is our future hope as believers. We will be given new bodies that no longer ache and new hearts that cannot sin because they have been perfected in the presence of God.

As we await that day, we trust that the same God—Redeemer, Restorer, Healer of hearts—is here with us now as our Sustainer. Whether we've truly blown it or we're simply having a rough day due to circumstances beyond our control, we can keep coming to our God who makes all things new. He loves to hear our prayers, and he is delighted to create right spirits within us. This is good news for the midnight hours, our failed moments, and every minute between.

TRANSFORMING A ROUGH DAY

Practically speaking, how do you turn a bad day around? Here are a few ideas that have worked for us.

1. *We get on our knees together.* If warranted, I look in my children's eyes and ask for their forgiveness. Then I say, "We're having a rough day, aren't we? Will you take a minute to pray with me?" We recognize that (a) the enemy would love to steal, kill, and destroy all the truth, beauty, and goodness being shared in our home, and (b) more often than not, the problem is not outside us—it originates in our hearts. We need the Lord's constant help to battle sin and live in unity with one another. Praying together is unifying and powerful to change the posture of our hearts and, therefore, our whole day.

2. *We speak the truth out loud.* One of our favorite scriptures to recall on hard days is Lamentations 3:22-23: "The steadfast love of the LORD never ceases; his mercies never come to an end; they are new every morning; great is your faithfulness." God's faithfulness, not our own, carries us through tough days.

3. *We do something out of the ordinary.* When the day feels like it's falling apart, we might end our homeschool lessons early and bake cookies together. We may pull out the art supplies, play a board game, or take a walk outside. It might feel counterintuitive to lean into your children when no one is getting along, but it might be exactly what is needed.

When Your Thoughts
Feel Like a Battlefield

THE LORD IS YOUR SUSTAINER

You keep him in perfect peace whose mind is
stayed on you, because he trusts in you.

ISAIAH 26:3

It's 2:00 a.m., and you're wide awake. Maybe this season at home with young children isn't as full of wonder and magic as you had imagined, and you're replaying your failures from the day. Or perhaps you feel all-consuming anxiety over mounting bills, a strained marriage, or a frightening diagnosis. You lie awake with tight shoulders and restless legs, gripped by fear.

Second Timothy 1:7 tells us that God has not given us a spirit of fear but one of power, love, and self-control. He has given us sound minds, but sin has upset and confused our thinking. Instead of experiencing peace and trust because we know we belong to God, our thought life can feel like a battlefield.

But because of our union with Christ (Ephesians 1:3-14), our hearts can be anchored to the promises of God, even when the dragons of 2:00 a.m. begin to roar. To combat the fear and anxiety that threaten to devour our joy, we must know and rehearse God's Word.

But it is not enough to merely know it. We must also *draw near* to the living Word, his presence, through prayer. In John 8:31-32, Jesus made this promise: "If you abide in my word, you are truly my disciples, and you will know the truth, and the truth will set you free." I have found this to be true: when I meditate on God's Word and offer it back to him in prayer, he releases me from worry and doubt, freeing my mind and heart to truly rest.

One helpful place to begin is by memorizing and praying through Psalm 121, a psalm you are now familiar with. The truth of this psalm helps us shift our focus away from ourselves and our seemingly insurmountable "hills" and lift our eyes back to where they belong: our mighty God who sustains us.

As you remind your soul of who God is according to his Word, you take your thoughts captive and make them obedient to Christ (2 Corinthians 10:5). Whether relief is felt instantly or experienced slowly over time, we can be certain that God draws near to us every time we call (Psalm 145:18).

In addition, focusing on the goodness of God in even the smallest blessings has proven to be a powerful antidote to anxiety. When I'm overwhelmed by bad news, I take inventory of specific ways I've seen God's goodness, and I immediately feel calmer. For example, I remember the good gifts of my family members who have made my life so rich, my husband's well-worn Bible on his nightstand, and the sudden arrival of spring after a long winter. I recall the mercy and forgiveness I am shown every time I sin. No, not all is well in the world. But God is relentlessly good, and he is in control. Dear friend, lift your eyes to him as Lord over the battlefield of your mind.

SCRIPTURE FOR THE BATTLEFIELD

In addition to Psalm 121, if you need a verse or a passage of Scripture to combat fear, worry, and shame, and to help your heart cling to hope, here are a few I love. Post them on your mirror or place them on your nightstand, and preach to your soul the truth that sets you free.

- Psalm 62:5-8, when your weary heart needs to know God's power
- Psalm 91:14-16, when you need to be reminded of his protection
- Psalm 51:1-2, when your soul is weighed down by the guilt of your sin
- Isaiah 41:10, when you need to remember that he is with you
- Revelation 21:1-4, when you need to fix your eyes on your glorious future with Christ

BOOK RECOMMENDATION

Memorizing Scripture: The Basics, Blessings, and Benefits of Meditating on God's Word by Glenna Marshall

When It Feels Like Time Is Slipping Away

THE LORD IS YOUR SUSTAINER

Teach us to number our days that we may get a heart of wisdom.

PSALM 90:12

I have a quirky method for picking up the pieces of our day: I assign myself a certain number of tasks before calling it quits for the night, counting as I go.

Toss a towel in the laundry basket...one.

Start the dishwasher...two.

Put a stack of books away...three.

It might sound unconventional, but it works. Because I know I only have a limited number of tasks, the end is in sight, and I'm motivated to keep going until the house is tidy.

As I went about my work the other night, a poignant truth dawned on me—these *days* are numbered too. There will come a day when I pull the last tiny pair of socks from the dryer or we read the final chapter of our read-aloud together. One day, we'll send our youngest child into the big wide world, and the house will grow quiet. Let's be honest: no one can prepare you for just how arduous some days can be. But the years fly by swiftly, don't they?

During a recent visit with my parents, my mom unveiled a treasure—a handwritten journal that had once belonged to my great-grandmother in the early 1940s. I cherished the opportunity to thumb through its yellowed pages, immersing myself in my great-grandmother's world through her own words. I discovered that Myrtle Ware was a woman of great depth: a seminary-educated teacher, a mother of four boys, and a devoted pastor's wife.

As I pored over her words, I was struck by the tension she felt during young motherhood and how closely it resembled my own, even though we are living 80 years apart. She grappled with the decision to step away from her beloved teaching role to support her husband's pastoral work and care for her growing family. Ultimately, she concluded that God had called her to this particular work for a season. Consider this journal entry from 1942:

> I loved teaching so much and enjoyed working in a profession so much more than housekeeping, that I wonder sometimes why multitudes of women may go back to their professions and I not be allowed to go back to mine: and make money as they do. Yet my better sense tells me that it is better as it is. I work incessantly as a pastor's wife. There is no remuneration, but a compensation greater. I am here when the boys come in from school. The house is warm. There is something to eat. My presence gives them security. That brings no salary with it…but I hear across the years, "Take this child and raise it for me and I will give thee thy wages." The Lord pays me—and will. All too soon the lads will be gone. All too quickly the years of their youth will have fled from my hands. They will be finished products. They will have gone forth. God help me that I shall have no regrets.

At their heart, these words express Myrtle's longing to obey God in her life and calling. As she wrote this journal entry and wrestled with her desire to spend time outside her home alongside her conviction to stay near her boys, she was unaware that she would not live to see all her children into adulthood. Myrtle died after a short battle with breast cancer just a few years later, when her youngest son was only three years old.

Myrtle Ware saw time as a valuable gift the Lord had entrusted to her. Her story doesn't suggest we should all become stay-at-home moms—that isn't feasible or desirable for many of us. But all of us can pray the words of Psalm 143:10: "Teach me to do your will, for you are my God! Let your good Spirit lead me on level ground!"

None of us knows what tomorrow holds or how many more tasks the Lord has assigned to us. Each day, in both big and small routines, we inhabit a tension: faithfully discerning what is required in the present, while not lamenting the past. After all, motherhood doesn't end when the baby clothes are boxed up, the training wheels come off, or even when our youngest child graduates from high school. If we are parenting children who place their trust in him, we are raising our spiritual brothers and sisters whom we will know and love for eternity. When it feels like time is slipping away, lift your eyes to your Sustainer God who holds your days in his hand and promises to lead you until the very end.

When You Need to Remember the Hope of the Resurrection

THE LORD IS YOUR SUSTAINER

*As Christians, we cannot escape the happy ending
no matter how far from our sight it is today.*

CINDY ROLLINS[1]

I t's tempting to despair at the state of the world—just watching the chaos on the news can trigger a state of panic if we let it. But in reality, we need not look beyond our four walls to feel the weight of sin and the wreckage it has caused in our lives: a troubled marriage, a child who has lost his way, our own stubborn hearts.

As I watched my children play in the creek today, unaware of the broken world around them, I was reminded of these powerful words:

This is my Father's world:
Oh, let me ne'er forget
That though the wrong seems oft so strong,
God is the ruler yet.[2]

When we need to lift our eyes to the end of the story to remember the hope that is ours, we can turn to the examples set by the people listed in Hebrews 12. This chapter of the Bible, often called the Hall of Faith, tells the stories of men and women who lifted their eyes to the Lord. They trusted in God's character and his promises, even in the face of dire circumstances, including enduring war and oppressive regimes, wandering through deserts, and dying the brutal death of a martyr. Did any of them receive what was promised to them during their lifetime? No, not even one. But they kept their eyes on the prize, looking beyond their current circumstances and acknowledging that they were strangers and exiles on this earth. They focused not on what was right in front of them, but on what they saw with eyes of faith—their eternal home. Fixing their eyes on the hope of eternity helped them endure their darkest moments.

But how do we know that a good and glorious end of the story awaits us? The answer lies in Christ's resurrection. Because he was raised, we can trust that all his other promises will be fulfilled as well. The resurrection is the receipt that proves all our debt has been paid and that everything that Jesus said will come true.[3]

On the morning of the resurrection, Mary Magdalene stood outside Jesus's tomb, crying. She looked inside the empty tomb, disturbed that someone had taken Jesus's body away. Mary had walked closely with Jesus throughout his ministry, and in her limited view, this was not how the story was supposed to end. Suddenly, the risen Jesus appeared before her, but she did not recognize him at first—her own grief and confusion naturally consumed her. But the moment Jesus spoke her name, she immediately knew her Lord and was filled with hope (John 20).

Have you ever felt like Mary? When we're right in the middle of a valley, it can be hard for us to see the bigger picture, and we may be disappointed by what we *can* see. But if we listen closely to God's Word and Spirit, we will hear him calling us by name and speaking his gentle love over us.

Two thousand years ago, the news of Jesus's resurrection brought great hope and joy to his followers. Two thousand years later, it should do the same for us! Because he was raised from the dead, we will one day be raised and will enjoy eternity with him.

Knowing that our Savior has triumphed over death and is coming again, just as he promised, offers us a living hope in the midst of the valleys we walk through in life. Today, you may face the harsh reality of a broken body, fractured relationships, or a wounded heart. But no matter how dark this day feels, if you are in Christ, you will one day stand before your God, face-to-face, and he will wipe every tear from your eyes.

Jesus is alive. There is hope! Lift up your eyes, sister. He is coming back soon!

When Your Cup Overflows

*Surely goodness and mercy shall follow me all the days of my
life, and I shall dwell in the house of the LORD forever.*

PSALM 23:6

As I glance through photos and journal entries from my first year as a mother of four, I see a weary woman. At that time, I wasn't getting more than a few hours of sleep in one stretch, was working odd hours at the hospital as a nurse, and was also attempting to homeschool our oldest two children with a toddler underfoot and a baby on my hip. I found it nearly impossible to lift my gaze beyond the immediate needs of my children—sleepless nights, constant diaper changes, tantrums—to imagine that motherhood would ever become easier or more enjoyable than it was at that moment. In addition, I had a limited perspective on my role as a disciple-maker in the grand scheme of eternity.

But looking back, I realize those days were fleeting, as all seasons are. We are now in the phase of parenting children who are in the sweet spot between diapers and driving. Our days are still full, but we are enjoying a good night's sleep. More importantly, we are witnessing spiritual growth in our children and grasping the true purpose of parenthood: guiding our kids to know, love, trust, and obey Jesus.

Our loving Father invites us to enjoy his good gifts in every season, not pining for the past or dreading the days to come. He asks us to be present in the moment and entrust our future to him.

Throughout this devotional, we've navigated many of the valleys of motherhood. But all mothers can attest that there are mountaintop moments as well, days your cup overflows. The first time your child says "I love you" without being prompted or brings you a handful of wilted wildflowers? A taste of heaven. The day your son or daughter places their faith in Jesus Christ for salvation? Indescribable joy! These moments call for true celebration.

In C.S. Lewis's novel *The Horse and His Boy*, a young boy named Shasta endures a perilous journey. Toward the end of the story, Shasta falls behind and becomes separated from his companions. He feels discouraged and defeated and calls himself "the most unfortunate boy that ever lived." But he soon realizes that he is not alone. A Voice speaks to him, revealing that he has been watching over and guiding him all along so that Shasta could fulfill his purpose of saving Narnia and Archenland. "There was only one lion," the Voice says. "I was the cat who comforted you among the houses of the dead. I was the lion who drove the jackals from you while you slept. I was the lion who gave the Horses the new strength of fear for the last mile so that you should reach King Lune in time. And I was the lion you do not remember who pushed the boat in which you lay, a child near death, so that it came to shore where a man sat, wakeful at midnight, to receive you."[1] Aslan, the Great Lion, had been intimately involved in Shasta's life as protector, provider, and comforter, even though Shasta had not been aware of his presence.

The same is true for us. One day, years from now, you'll look back on your most challenging days as a mom and recognize God's hand was at work in a thousand different ways: comforting, shepherding, sustaining, and providing for you. He never left your side. He was always there. But even as we look to our past and are comforted by his presence, we can also look to the future and rejoice in what he is preparing for us. The prophet Isaiah gives us a glimpse of the joy that awaits us:

> On this mountain the Lord of hosts will make for all peoples a feast of rich food, a feast of well-aged wine, of rich food full of marrow, of aged wine well refined. And he will swallow up on this mountain the covering that is cast over all peoples, the veil that is spread over all nations. He will swallow up death forever; and the Lord God will wipe away tears from all faces, and the reproach of his people he will take away from all the earth, for the Lord has spoken. It will be said on that day, "Behold, this is our God; we have waited for him, that he might save us. This is the Lord; we have waited for him; let us be glad and rejoice in his salvation (Isaiah 25:6-9).

Maybe you're in the trenches or running on empty as you read these words. Hang on, friend. Don't lose hope. Hold tightly to God's promise never to leave or forsake you, because he never will. Whether here on earth or in heaven, the dark valleys you're walking through will transform into mountaintops of joy as you lift your eyes to the one who was, and is, and is to come!

> *The Lord bless you and keep you; the Lord make his face*
> *to shine upon you and be gracious to you; the Lord lift*
> *up his countenance upon you and give you peace.*
>
> NUMBERS 6:24-26

Lift your eyes to behold and worship him: your Help, Provider, the God who sees you, your Protector, Keeper, Comfort, Shepherd, and Sustainer.

Recommended Resources
on the Psalms

Walter Brueggemann and William H. Bellinger Jr., *Psalms* (Cambridge: Cambridge University Press, 2014).

Derek Kidner, *Psalms 73-150: An Introduction and Commentary: No. 15 Tyndale Old Testament Commentaries* (Downers Grove, IL: IVP, 2014).

Tremper Longman, *Psalms: An Introduction and Commentary: 15 Tyndale Old Testament Commentaries* (Downers Grove, IL: IVP, 2014).

Alec Motyer, *Psalms by the Day: A New Devotional Translation* (Christian Focus, 2016).

Eugene Peterson, *A Long Obedience in the Same Direction: Discipleship in an Instant Society* (Downers Grove, IL: IVP, 1980; 2019).

O. Palmer Robertson, *The Flow of the Psalms: Discovering Their Structure and Theology* (Phillipsburg, NJ: P & R Publishing, 2015).

Notes

Dedication

1. This dedication is adapted and borrowed from our former pastor, Ray Ortlund. He used this as a call to worship before Sunday services.

Introduction

1. James Montgomery Boice, *Psalms: Volume 3, Psalms 107-150* (Grand Rapids: Baker Books, 1998), 1075.

2. See Avraham Yeshaya Hotzberg, "Conduct During Childbirth," TheJewishWoman.org, accessed June 26, 2024, https://www.chabad.org/theJewishWoman/article_cdo/aid/72288/jewish/Con duct-During-Childbirth.htm and "Shir Hamalos," Mikrah.org, accessed June 26, 2024, https://www.mikvah.org/article/shir_hamalos.

When You Know You're Not Enough

1. John Newton, *One Hundred and Twenty-Nine Letters from the Rev. John Newton to Josiah Bull*, ed. William Bull (London: Hamilton, Adams, and Co., 1847), 192. This letter was written on February 21, 1784. As quoted in Tony Reinke, *Newton on the Christian Life: To Live Is Christ* (Wheaton: Crossway, 2015), 228.

2. Timothy J. Keller, *The New City Catechism: 52 Questions and Answers for Our Hearts and Minds* (Wheaton: Crossway, 2017), 16-17.

When You Need to Remember That God Will Provide

1. Charles H. Spurgeon, *The Treasury of David: Classic Reflections on the Wisdom of the Psalms* (Peabody: Hendrickson Publishers, 2022), 34.

2. "George Müller: Trusting God for Daily Bread," Mission Minded Families, accessed June 26, 2024, https://www.missionmindedfamilies.org/blog/muller.

When It's Hard to Keep Giving and Serving

1. L.B. Cowman, *Streams in the Desert* (Grand Rapids: Zondervan, 1997), 425.

2. Michael Farren, Jonny Robinson, and Rich Thompson, *Yet Not I But Through Christ In Me* © 2018 Integrity's Alleluia! Music (SESAC), Farren Love and War Publishing (SESAC), City-Alight Music (APRA) (all adm at IntegratedRights.com). Lyrics reprinted with permission.

When You're Angry

1. Sinclair B. Ferguson, *The Dawn of Redeeming Grace: Daily Devotions for Advent* (Epsom, UK: The Good Book Company, 2021), 146.

When You Need to Remember Who You Are in Christ

1. Tim Keller with Kathy Keller, *The Meaning of Marriage: Facing the Complexities of Commitment with the Wisdom of God* (New York: Penguin Publishing Group, 2013), 44.

2. C.S. Lewis, *The Lion, the Witch and the Wardrobe* (New York: Harper Collins, 1950), 141.

When You're Afraid of the Future

1. Elisabeth Elliot, *Keep a Quiet Heart* (Grand Rapids: Revell, 2006), 53.

When You Cannot Sleep Because of Worry

1. Matthew Henry, *Matthew Henry's Commentary on the Whole Bible*, Vol. 5, commentary on Matthew 8 Verses 23-27, available online on at https://m.egwwritings.org/en/book/14192.21421 #21429.

When You Battle Discontentment

1. Jim Elliot, quoted in Elisabeth Elliot, *The Journals of Jim Elliot* (Grand Rapids: Revell, 2004), 278.

Part Five: The Lord Is Your Keeper

1. Charles H. Spurgeon, *The Treasury of David: Classic Reflections on the Wisdom of the Psalms* (Peabody: Hendrickson Publishers, 2022), 15.

When the Days Feel Mundane

1. Charles H. Spurgeon, *The Metropolitan Tabernacle Pulpit Sermons*, "Strengthening Medicine for God's Servants," vol. 21, no. 1,214 (London: Passmore & Alabaster, 1875), 54.

When You Feel Ashamed for How You've Failed as a Mom

1. John Bunyan, *The Pilgrim's Progress* (Oxford: Oxford University Press, 2009), 37.

When You're Tempted Toward Laziness

1. Popularized by Elisabeth Elliot and written by Mrs. George A. Paull, this poem was originally published by Eleanor Amerman Sutphen in a book called *Ye Nexte Thynge* (New York: Revell, 1897), 1-2.
2. Paull, "The Next Thing."

When You Need to Remember Your Purpose

1. Charles H. Spurgeon, *The Metropolitan Tabernacle Pulpit Sermons,* "A Sermon and a Reminiscence," vol. 54, no. 3112, see https://www.spurgeon.org/resource-library/sermons/a-sermon-and-a-reminiscence/#flipbook/.
2. Gloria Furman, *Missional Motherhood: The Everyday Ministry of Motherhood in the Grand Plan of God* (Wheaton: Crossway, 2016), 186.

When Life Isn't Going as You Planned

1. Timothy Keller, *Prayer: Experiencing Awe and Intimacy with God* (New York: Penguin Books, 2014), 228.
2. Robert J. Morgan, *Then Sings My Soul* (Nashville: Thomas Nelson, 2003), 207.
3. George Matheson wrote *O Love That Will Not Let Me Go* in 1882. This hymn is now in the public domain.

When You're Tempted to Compare

1. The author of this hymn is unknown, and these lyrics are now in the public domain. For the full lyrics, see https://www.pdhymns.com/pdh_main_Children.htm.
2. This line is from William Blake's 1804 Poem, "Milton," available from the William Blake Archive, https://blakearchive.org/work/milton.

When You're Suffering and Need to Know God Is Near

1. Lilias Trotter wrote this line in her journal on August 1, 1901, while serving as a missionary in North Africa.

2. Darlene Deibler Rose, *Evidence Not Seen: A Woman's Miraculous Faith in the Jungles of World War II* (New York: Harper Collins, 1990), 46.

When You Struggle to Love Your Children Well

1. Tim Kimmel, *Grace-Based Parenting* (Nashville: Thomas Nelson, 2005), 111.

Part Seven: The Lord Is Your Shepherd

1. David Gibson, *The Lord of Psalm 23: Jesus Our Shepherd, Companion, and Host* (Wheaton: Crossway, 2023), 17.
2. Charles H. Spurgeon, *The Treasury of David: Classic Reflections on the Wisdom of the Psalms* (Peabody: Hendrickson Publishers, 2022), 16.

When You Doubt Your Ability to Mother Well

1. "Shrek the Sheep Faces His Shearers," BBC News, April 19, 2004, news.bbc.co.uk/2/hi/asia-pacific/3639315.stm.

When Your Affections for God Feel Weak

1. David Gibson, *The Lord of Psalm 23: Jesus Our Shepherd, Companion, and Host* (Wheaton: Crossway, 2023), 44.
2. Tara-Leigh Cobble, *The Bible Recap: A One-Year Guide to Reading and Understanding the Entire Bible* (Bloomington: Bethany House, 2020). You can also find free resources to help you read and understand the Bible at www.thebiblerecap.com.

When Church Hurts

1. Martin Luther, in *Luther's Works* (St. Louis, 1957), XXII:55.
2. Timothy Keller, *The Prodigal God: Recovering the Heart of the Christian Faith* (New York: Penguin Books, 2011), 127.

Part Eight: The Lord Is Your Sustainer

1. Charles H. Spurgeon, *The Treasury of David: Classic Reflections on the Wisdom of the Psalms* (Peabody: Hendrickson Publishers, 2022), 24.

When You Need to Remember the Hope of the Resurrection

1. Cindy Rollins, *Beyond Mere Motherhood: Moms are People Too* (Wichita: Blue Sky Daisies LLC, 2023), 204.
2. "This Is My Father's World" was written by Maltbie D. Babcock in 1901. It is now in public domain.
3. I heard this perspective on the resurrection in a sermon by my pastor, Ryan Welsh, given on Easter Sunday 2024 at Restoration Church, Southlake, Texas. See https://www.restorationtx.com/sermons?sapurl=Lyt0ZnhuL21lZGlhL21pLytycXR0d3luP2VtYmVkPXRydWUmcmVjZW50Um91dGU9YXBwLndlYi1hcHAuGlicmFyeS5saXXN0J nJlY2VudFJvdXRlU2x1Zz0lMkI1dmt2M3J6.

When Your Cup Overflows

1. C.S. Lewis, *The Horse and His Boy* (New York: C.S. Lewis Pte. Ltd., 1954), 164-165.

Acknowledgments

To my precious Lord and Savior, Jesus Christ, you have been my Help from my very first breath and you promise to walk me all the way home. The time I've spent writing this devotional has been such sweet communion with you. I love you.

Thank you to my dear husband, Shawn, who has kept his covenant to pursue Christ and to pursue me. You made writing this book in a busy season not only possible but enjoyable. Thank you for pushing me out the door to write and for adding gospel clarity to every page. I love you and am so grateful and proud to be yours!

To my children—Liam, Lanie, Bear, and Beckham—I will never stop praising God for the unspeakable joy you bring to my life. You are my treasures.

To the vibrant community of Brighter Day Press moms, you spur me on every day with your fervor for Christ and devotion to your families. I pray that this book serves as a discipleship tool for you who are learning, as I am, to shift your gaze from the needs right in front of you to the steadfast love of the Lord.

Thank you to Sally Clarkson, who has mentored me from afar and has given me a powerful vision for motherhood through her faithful speaking and writing. Sally, what an exceptional honor to have the foreword of this book about motherhood written by you.

Thank you to my parents, Dick and Mel Tunney, who taught me to "dream in color" and never shied away from even the most extravagant dreams (like writing and illustrating a book). You were my first window into the character of Christ, and I'm thankful for how you have modeled a life marked by lifting your eyes to him.

Thank you to my grandma, Janet Tunney, who has been my sounding board and one of my best friends for over three decades. I hope you read these words and grasp how your faithful example has impacted so many of them.

Thank you to Erin Miller for tapping me on the shoulder, inviting me to lunch on my first Sunday in Texas, and becoming my lifelong friend. Your belief in the value of this book and feedback along the way made it possible.

To Kirra Sutton and Whitney Winkler, your constant friendship through so many stages of life has been a source of comfort, and I am shaped by your wisdom.

Thank you to Nina Treat, who handled much of the behind-the-scenes of Brighter Day Press and loved our community so well as I spent time writing. Your encouragement is an unmerited gift.

To Ilene Butler, thank you for your daily voice messages that spurred me on in the writing of this book. Some days, your truth-filled words and insightful edits were exactly what I needed to keep going.

Thank you to Audrey Greeson, Bob Hawkins Jr., and Harvest House Publishers, who saw the potential of this book before I did. Thank you for taking a chance on me and for helping me navigate the journey of writing my first book.

To Jenna Brack, your insightful editing work has added immeasurable depth and clarity. I am so grateful for the heart and skill you poured into this project.

Finally, thank you to my local church, Restoration Church in Southlake, Texas, for your friendship, accountability, and sharpening; and to my pastor, Ryan Welsh, for faithfully preaching God's Word.